# THE
# SECRET
# LIBRARY

# THE
# SECRET
# LIBRARY

## A Book Lover's Journey
## Through Curiosities of Literature

# OLIVER TEARLE

Michael O'Mara Books Limited

This paperback edition first published in 2024
First published in Great Britain in 2016 by
Michael O'Mara Books Limited
9 Lion Yard
Tremadoc Road
London SW4 7NQ

A CIP catalogue record for this book is
available from the British Library.

This product is made of material from well-
managed, FSC®-certified forests and other controlled
sources. The manufacturing processes conform to the
environmental regulations of the country of origin.

ISBN: 978-1-78929-592-4 in paperback print format
ISBN: 978-1-78243-558-7 in ebook format

1 2 3 4 5 6 7 8 9 10

Jacket design by Anna Morrison
Designed and typeset by Claire Cater

Printed and bound by CPI Group (UK) Ltd, Croydon, CR0 4YY

www.mombooks.com

# CONTENTS

# INTRODUCTION

When asked once what book he'd like to have with him on a desert island, G. K. Chesterton replied: '*Thomas's Guide to Practical Shipbuilding.*' Such a witty retort probably raised smiles but meant he never got invited back onto *Desert Island Discs*. Yet Chesterton's quip does remind us of the plain but often forgotten fact that 'book' needn't mean 'great work of literature' or 'novel you've always wanted to read but have never had the time or courage to take on'. A book can be of an altogether more pragmatic kind, yet its importance to the history of Western society might be extensive.

Take Euclid's *Elements*, a classical textbook written over two thousand years ago. Few bookworms probably take Euclid to bed with them after a long day at work, but the influence of the *Elements* is immeasurable (somewhat ironically, given its subject). Similarly, few readers probably sink into a hot bath with Dr Johnson's *Dictionary* of an evening, but every dictionary written since, from *Webster's* in America to the astounding achievement that is the *Oxford English Dictionary*, owes some sort of debt to it. Such books reflect the age that produced them but have also helped to shape the course of cultural and intellectual development ever since. That is what this book is about.

Indeed, *The Secret Library* sets out to explore, and to attempt answers to, some of the book-related questions I've been curious about for a while. Some of them are questions I've already attempted to answer on my blog, *Interesting Literature: A Library of Literary Interestingness*. But most of them, especially those involving non-literary texts, are new to this book. What *did* Euclid do that was so groundbreaking and important? Has science fiction ever accurately predicted the future? Who wrote the first cookbook? Were the Victorians really a bunch of prudes – and were their novels truly shy around the trouser area?

*The Secret Library* tries to find answers to these and other questions. It has two related aims: to bring to light the lesser-known aspects of well-known books, and to show how obscure and little-known books have surprising links with the familiar world around us. It seeks strangeness within the familiar, and familiarity within what is otherwise strange. In short, it attempts to bring to light some hidden facts about both the best-known and the least-known books ever written, typed, inscribed, dictated or, indeed, fabricated.

Dig a bit deeper into the world of books, and you find all sorts of untold stories. Everyone's heard of the classical Greek poet Homer, but what about the writers who parodied him? Edgar Allan Poe's short stories are justly celebrated, but few know the rather surprising book – indeed, the *only* one of his books – that sold well in his own lifetime. We all know that Shakespeare wrote a play called *Hamlet*, but he wasn't the first playwright to do so. It is with such overlooked books, which have slipped behind the back of the library shelves and become largely forgotten, that this book is particularly concerned. But sometimes a well-thumbed tome comes under the spotlight too: I wouldn't claim that Dante's *Divine Comedy* was an obscure book, but how many people have actually read it? Consequently, its more, er, *flatulent* moments are one of medieval literature's best-kept secrets.

*The Secret Library* is not intended as a list of the ninety-nine most influential books ever written or a compilation of 'ninety-nine books everyone should read' – not least because several of the books I discuss haven't survived into the modern age, and one of them probably never even existed in the first place. (All will be explained in due course.) Instead, it's a medley of curiosities, a whistle-stop tour around an imaginary library stuffed full of titles both familiar and forgotten. Each of the books I discuss tells us something about the age that produced it. And, collectively, they provide some intriguing answers to the questions I just mentioned.

This book is organized into nine chapters, roughly covering the major historical and cultural periods from antiquity to the present day: the ancient world, the Middle Ages, the Renaissance, and so on. After the mid-seventeenth century everything became a bit more interesting and complicated, not least because a new land known as America began to publish books at this time. I tell the history of America's bookish development over the seventeenth, eighteenth and nineteenth centuries in a separate chapter; the same goes for similar developments on the Continent. Everyone regroups for the final chapter, which takes the twentieth-century age of Western modernity as its focus.

One final thing before we embark on our library tour. In each of the nine chapters, every single entry is linked to the previous one in some way. Sometimes the connections between two books will be obvious; sometimes they will take a bit longer to discern. But they are there. I hope you enjoy looking for them as much as I did.

*Oliver Tearle*

# THE CLASSICAL WORLD

The legacy of the classical world is all around us: democracy, theatre, lyric poetry, the Olympics and a fair bit of philosophy and architecture have their roots in ancient Greece. But on a smaller level, too, we inhabit a world created by our classical forebears. Take the language we use, such as the Latin phrases still in common use: *carpe diem* ('seize the day', from the poet Horace) or *in vino veritas* ('in wine there is truth', from Pliny the Elder). In England until 2017, most people carried a piece of *The Aeneid* about with them every day: the line *decus et tutamen* ('an ornament and a safeguard'), taken from Virgil's poem, was inscribed around the edges of pound coins. American money, too, bears a Latin phrase: *E pluribus unum* ('out of the many, one') dates back to another text that has been attributed to Virgil. (Pleasingly, it's a pesto recipe.)

This is all the more impressive since many works of classical literature, philosophy, science and mathematics haven't survived. Just imagine if some of the classical works that didn't make it into the modern age were still with us. Think what riches we would possess if we had all one hundred or so of Sophocles' plays, rather than the mere seven that have been preserved. Nobody can study Aristotle's theory of comedy, the second part of his book the *Poetics*, on a university literature course, for the simple reason that no copy of the work has survived.

Given that books are the bread and butter of the book you now hold, it seems fitting to begin with the ancient world, since it was there that the book itself was effectively invented. The oldest book comprising multiple pages (that is, not simply a big scroll) is often said to be the Etruscan Gold Book, which was produced around 2,500 years ago. It comprises six large sheets of 24-carat gold which have been bound together with rings, thus forming a unified object that might be labelled a 'book'. It was only discovered in the mid-twentieth century; unfortunately, as it was written in the Etruscan language, which we know very little about, deciphering it proved tricky, to say the least. To this day, we have no idea what it says.

Fortunately, there are many works of poetry, drama, fiction, science and philosophy that we *can* decipher and read. So, rather than scratching our heads over the impenetrable oddities of Etruscan script, let's have a look at some of those.

## ✧ Homer's Epic ✧

We know Homer for two epic poems: the *Iliad*, about the Trojan War, and the *Odyssey*, about what Odysseus did on his way home to Ithaca. The *Iliad* is the first great work of Western literature, probably composed in around the eighth century

BCE. It recounts the ten-year Trojan War between Troy and a number of Greek states, with a particular focus on the final moments of the conflict. It features everything from fearsome Amazons (warrior women whom Homer calls 'antianeirai', which has been translated as 'equals of men') to conquering heroes such as Agamemnon and Achilles. And that's all just things beginning with the letter A.

Who 'Homer' was remains a mystery. We're not even entirely certain when he lived, assuming that he did at all. The precise nature of the composition of the *Iliad* also remains something of a mystery: the poem probably started out as part of an oral tradition and was only written down much later, but whether Homer was the blind bard of legend remains unknown – and, after nearly three millennia, unknowable.

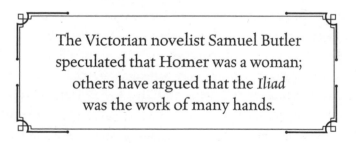

The Victorian novelist Samuel Butler speculated that Homer was a woman; others have argued that the *Iliad* was the work of many hands.

The stories in the Trojan War have found their way into numerous aspects of our daily lives. The story of the Greeks cunningly entering their enemies' city disguised in a big wooden horse inspired the *Trojan horse* (in computing, a piece of malware that infiltrates your computer by disguising itself as something benign). The character of Hector gave us the verb *to hector*, meaning to harass or bully someone. And if we wish to draw attention to the one weakness of an otherwise seemingly invincible person we still refer to their *Achilles' heel*, after the one weak portion of that Greek hero's anatomy. (Curiously, though, Homer makes no mention of this story, which appears to have been a later invention. Indeed, in the *Iliad* Achilles is not exactly invulnerable: at one point, a spear hits him in the elbow and draws blood.)

The one thing everyone thinks they know about the *Iliad* isn't quite true: namely, that it tells of the war between the Trojans and the Greeks. As Richard Jenkyns points out in his book *Classical Literature*, they didn't consider themselves 'Greek', which was a later appellation used by the Romans. They called themselves Hellenes, but even this is inaccurate in relation to the *Iliad*, where Homer calls them Achaeans, Argives or Danaans – but never Greeks or Hellenes. What's more, while the Trojan War lasted for ten years, Homer's *Iliad* covers only a few weeks in the final stage of the war – and twenty-two of the twenty-four books which make up the poem cover the events of just a few days.

In classical times 'Homer' was named as the author of several other works besides the *Iliad* and the *Odyssey*, among them a comic poem called *Margites*, after its monumentally silly protagonist. Margites is mad, pedantic, vain, and above all, stupid – so stupid that he doesn't know which of his parents gave birth to him. Although most of the poem has not survived, we know that it enjoyed considerable popularity during classical times. A philosopher named Philodemus uses the phrase 'mad as Margites' in his writings. The line attributed to many writers and thinkers since – about the fox knowing many things, but the hedgehog knowing one big thing – originates in *Margites*.

But did Homer write *Margites*? Scholars are doubtful. No less an authority than Aristotle attributed the poem to Homer in his *Poetics*, but others have taken the attribution with a pinch of salt, putting forward another Greek writer, Pigres, as a more probable claimant for the authorship. Another poem which Aristotle attributed to Homer, but which historians have since ascribed to a variety of other poets, is *Batrachomyomachia*, which translates as 'The Battle of Frogs and Mice'. It's essentially one giant spoof of Homer's *Iliad*, with the Greeks and Trojans replaced by amphibians and rodents, and the author poking fun at the heroics of the *Iliad*. Right from the start – or very near the start, anyway – Western literature was sending itself up.

In *Batrachomyomachia* the Frog King is giving the Mouse King a lift across a pond, when suddenly they spot a water-snake. In order to protect himself, the Frog King instinctively dives underwater, jettisoning the Mouse King from his back in the process. The poor Mouse King drowns, and his people (sorry, his mice) interpret the Frog King's actions as wilful murder, and vow revenge on the Frog King and his people (sorry, his frogs).

George Chapman, the Elizabethan poet, translated the *Batrachomyomachia* into English, but Keats probably wasn't thinking of the frog-and-mouse poem when he penned his sonnet 'On First Looking into Chapman's Homer'. Still, the mock-epic appears to challenge the portrayal of war in Homer's *Iliad*, which, although it also highlights the futility of war, clothes the Trojan War as a whole in grandeur and heroism. War in the *Batrachomyomachia* is nothing but a petty squabble. As well as being one of the first comic poems, it may also qualify as the first anti-war poem.

# Fabulous Aesop

The tradition of using animals in literature was already firmly established when Pigres – or whoever was its actual author – composed the *Batrachomyomachia*. But animal stories could be used for moral instruction as well as for bathetic comic effect. The clearest example of this can be found in Aesop's *Fables*. One of his fables even begins with a frog carrying a mouse across a pond, only to drown it midway.

> According to Plato's *Phaedo*, Socrates whiled away his time in prison composing poems based on Aesop's fables.

Aesop wasn't the first person to write animal fables. Several centuries earlier, Hesiod had written one about a hawk and a nightingale, while a poet named Archilochus penned several, including one about an eagle and a vixen, and another about a fox and a monkey. But Aesop would turn the fable into a popular form. William Caxton printed the first English translation of the *Fables* in 1484, enabling such phrases as 'sour grapes' and 'to cry wolf' to enter the language – though not, as is sometimes claimed, 'a wolf in sheep's clothing'. (Although one of Aesop's *Fables* does feature a wolf who dresses as a sheep, this is actually a biblical phrase.) Other phrases gifted us by the *Fables* have been misinterpreted, or creatively reinvented at any rate: 'the lion's share', for instance, comes from one of the fables in which the lion takes *all* of the food, leaving the rest of his hunting party with no share of the spoils. Now, we use the 'lion's share' to mean simply the largest, and the bitter irony of Aesop's story is lost. Some of the lesser-known fables include 'The Mouse and the Oyster', 'The Man with Two Mistresses' and 'Washing the Ethiopian White'.

As with Homer, we can't be sure an 'Aesop' ever actually existed. If he did, it was probably in around the sixth century BCE, several centuries after Homer, if Homer himself ever existed. Aesop's *Fables* may have been the work of many hands, part of an oral tradition that gradually accumulated. Nevertheless, legends grew up around the storyteller. One commentator claimed that Aesop fought at the battle of Thermopylae in 480 BCE, but since by then he had been dead for nearly a century one can't imagine he was much help.

Indeed, if a man named Aesop did exist in the first place, he is thought to have been a disabled black slave. The idea that he was of African descent – possibly from Ethiopia – dates back some time. The presence of such animals as camels and elephants in the fables, not to mention the tale 'Washing the Ethiopian White', support this theory. The conjecture of his Ethiopian descent comes not only from the fable about the Ethiopian but also his name: according to one scholar, Maximos Planudes, Aesop (or Esop) comes from 'Ethiop'. (Note: it probably doesn't.)

Whatever the derivation of his name, the theory that Aesop was a slave makes a certain amount of sense in light of his fables. A man of such a low social status in Greek society would not be able to speak his mind: if he was lucky enough to be able to read and write, he would have to write allegorically about the society he lived in. Aristotle and Herodotus both support the 'slave' hypothesis, enabling literary historians to conjecture that Aesop was a slave on the island of Samos. A popular story first told by Plutarch has Aesop meeting his end in Delphi, where he is thrown from a cliff having been found guilty of stealing, but most historians dismiss this as fiction.

If fables are stories with a moral, what are the morals of Aesop's *Fables*? The most famous is probably found in 'The Tortoise and the Hare', which advises that 'slow and steady wins the race'. But the fable invites other interpretations: its moral could also be that overconfidence leads one to waste one's talents (the hare, cocksure of his victory in the race, idiotically takes a nap halfway). Or, perhaps, a bit of both.

## ✧ The Poet of Lesbos ✧

Around the turn of the twentieth century, a series of excavations of a rubbish dump in the city of Oxyrhynchus in Egypt, about 100 miles south of Cairo, led to the discovery of some papyrus scrolls. They contained, among other things, some fragments of *Margites*, but also a fair bit of long-lost poetry by the lyric poet Sappho. We are still finding her poetry: two more fragments came to light in 2004 and 2012.

In his *Histories*, the Greek writer Herodotus connects Sappho with Aesop via Rhodopis, the Thracian courtesan whose life became the basis for the first version of the 'Cinderella' fairy tale. (The Greek word for such women was 'hetaerae' – high-class female companions for men with cash on the hip.) According to Herodotus, whom we should probably take with a generous pinch of salt, Rhodopis and Aesop were friends (if that is quite the word), and when Rhodopis was captured by an Egyptian pharaoh, it was Sappho's brother Charaxus who freed her 'with a great sum'. So, to get from Aesop to Sappho we have to go via the original Cinderella.

Although only a small amount of her poetry has survived, Sappho has had a posthumous literary reputation that most lyric poets can only dream of. And despite the tantalizingly little we know about her life or her writing – or perhaps *because* we know so little – she has become an icon for lyric poets, and, of course, a symbol for homosexual love between women. 'The female Homer' is one of the many sobriquets for her; Plato called her 'the tenth Muse'. The Victorian poet Algernon Charles Swinburne thought her the finest poet ever, better even than Homer or Shakespeare. Not bad for someone whose work mostly survives only as fragments.

> One scholar took the trouble to copy
> out one of Sappho's poems because
> he admired her use of vowels.

It wasn't always this way. Once there were abundant copies of Sappho's poems in circulation. But time's fell hand, along with various library fires and disapproving churchmen who didn't take kindly to the 'wanton' sexuality evident in the poems, put an end to that. By the Middle Ages, only a small portion of Sappho's poems survived. It would not be until 1904, when the

Canadian poet Bliss Carman published *Sappho: One Hundred Lyrics*, that the greatest female poet of antiquity would be published in an English translation of any substantial length. And even here, a fair bit of the poetry was not the work of Sappho but of Carman himself, who took it upon himself to add lines of verse to his translations. The book was a huge success, and helped set the trend for modern poetry, especially the Imagist verse of Ezra Pound, Hilda Doolittle (herself no stranger to Sapphic love), and others.

Sappho's life has also attracted much speculation, and we know less about that than we do about her poetry. She is the reason we talk of *lesbian* relationships between women, because of the homoerotic strain in her poems and because she hailed, of course, from the Greek island of Lesbos. 'Lesbian' is a relatively modern term: the earliest known instance of the word being used to describe homosexual women is in a 1925 letter by Aldous Huxley (who later wrote *Brave New World*), with 'Lesbianism' being attested from 1870 in the diary of the dirty Victorian poet Arthur Munby. Before the late nineteenth century, 'tribade' and 'tribadism' were the usual terms (from the Greek for 'to rub'). The arrival of 'lesbianism' on the scene coincides with growing interest in the work of Sappho. Its discovery changed not only the face of twentieth-century poetry but also the way we talk about same-sex female relationships.

## ⟡ Elementary ⟡

To an architect or stonemason, a 'Lesbian rule' is a ruler made of lead that can be bent to fit the curves of a building. The phrase also has a figurative sense, referring to a principle or opinion that is not fixed but can be reshaped or revised over time. It is thanks to Aristotle that we know the Greeks had Lesbian rules. (It's sometimes good to know these things.) In his *Nicomachean Ethics*, he refers to it in relation to justice: 'Lesbian builders', he writes, use a rule made of lead, 'for the rule is altered to suit the figure of the stone, and is not fixed, and so is a decree or decision to suit the circumstances.'

Although Aristotle wrote about mathematics as well as philosophy, probably the greatest mathematician of ancient Greece was Euclid. But which Euclid? There were, it would appear, several. Euclid of Megara was a pupil of Socrates who founded a school of philosophy; this Euclid was so devoted to his teacher that when Megara banned its citizens from travelling to Athens where Socrates taught, Euclid would sneak into Athens at night, dressed as a woman. None of the works of this Euclid have survived. The other Euclid, of Alexandria, is the famous one – and the one who wrote the book known as the *Elements*.

At least, it's assumed that Euclid wrote the *Elements*. The evidence is, in fact, slight. Many early copies don't mention its author. The attribution of the work to Euclid is the result of one passing reference made by a later writer, Proclus, naming Euclid as the author of the book. Still, most historians accept the attribution as fact.

> The first English translation of Euclid appeared in 1570, with a preface by John Dee, astrologer to Queen Elizabeth I.

*Elements* is not the oldest Greek mathematical work to have survived – another text, *On the Moving Sphere*, had been written by a man named Autolycus a generation earlier – but it's certainly the one that's wielded the most influence. It is almost unanimously regarded by scholars as the most influential textbook ever written. It was translated into Arabic in the ninth century and inspired a raft of mathematical discoveries in the Middle East over the next few centuries. After the Bible, it was the most widely printed book in medieval Europe. And yet it is among the most unread influential books, up there with Isaac Newton's *Principia* and Karl Marx's *Das Kapital*.

Much of the early parts of the book are often said to be based on the work of Pythagoras. Or at least, the work commonly attributed to Pythagoras. Pythagoras did many things: his views on the transmigration of souls would influence later philosophers including Plato, and his teachings on religious mysticism attracted a number of adherents. He left a series of commandments for his followers to observe, which promoted the importance of abstaining from beans, never urinating in the direction of the sun, and, perhaps oddest of all, not having children with a woman who wears gold jewellery. Legends grew up around him: he once even managed the impressive feat of being in two cities at the same time, according to one source. Just about the only thing he had nothing to do with was mathematics. His reputation as a great mathematician was another posthumous legend, cooked up by Speusippus and Xenocrates, two philosophers of Plato's Academy, in order to give the impression that Plato's own scientific ideas chimed with older, more established theories. The theorem about right-angled triangles that bears his name was only first attributed to him 500 years after his death.

Similarly, although the *Elements* is referred to as 'Euclid's *Elements*', and Euclid certainly wrote it, the amount of original work in the book is relatively small. It may even have been modelled on an earlier book, written by Hippocrates of Chios, which hasn't survived. But the fact that so much of the *Elements* draws on the work of others only reinforces its status as the Western world's first textbook. Euclid's great talent was in bringing together the theorems arrived at by other mathematicians and presenting the whole field of geometry and trigonometry in a clear and accessible style.

## ✧ Oedipus Complex ✧

Aristotle was an innovative and influential philosopher. He was also, after Plato, one of the first literary critics, at least the first whose work has survived. In his *Poetics* he gave us the first-ever work of what became known, in the twentieth century, as literary theory. In this work he muses on what makes a good tragedy, and decides that the most representative example of the genre is a play by Sophocles called *Oedipus Rex*.

Tragedy as a genre began in ancient Greece, and the first great tragedies were staged as part of a huge festival known as the City Dionysia. Thousands of Greek citizens would gather in the Theatre of Dionysus Eleuthereus to watch a trilogy of tragic plays, such as Aeschylus' *Oresteia*. Going to the theatre in ancient Greece was, socially speaking, closer to attending a football match than a modern-day theatre.

Because audiences were so vast, actors wore masks that symbolized their particular character, so even those sitting towards the back of the theatre could keep track of who was who. In Latin, the word for such a mask was *persona*, which is to this day why we talk about adopting a persona whenever we become someone else – we are, metaphorically if not literally, putting on a mask. This is also the reason why the list of characters in a play is known as the 'Dramatis Personae'.

The City Dionysia in Greece possibly grew out of earlier fertility festivals where plays would be performed, and a goat would be ritually sacrificed to the god of wine, fertility and crops, Dionysus. The idea was that the sacrificial goat would rid the city state of its sins, much as with the Judeo-Christian concept of the scapegoat. Tragedy, then, was designed to have a sort of purging effect upon the community – and this is even encoded within the word *tragedy* itself, which probably comes from the Greek for 'goat song'.

> The Oedipus story gave Sigmund Freud, father of psychoanalysis, the idea for his 'Oedipus complex', where every male child harbours an unconscious desire to do what Oedipus did.

One of the most celebrated tragedies of ancient Greece was *Oedipus Rex*, Sophocles' play about the Theban king who had unwittingly killed his father and married his mother, thus fulfilling a prophecy that he had spent his life trying to avert. In terms of genre, tragedy requires a tragic hero, one who is usually tempted to perform a deed (frequently, though not always, a murder). After the deed has been committed, the hero's fortunes suffer a decline, ending with his death or, in the case of *Oedipus Rex*, the (self-administered) putting-out of his eyes. (Freud read much into that, too, seeing it as a symbolic castration.)

The idea behind Greek tragedy, then, was to encourage the spectators to review their own thoughts and behaviour and make sure they avoided the same fate as Oedipus. Oedipus may have *inadvertently* killed his father and married his mother, but it was his pride that led him to enter into an altercation with Laius (the man who turned out to be his dad) in the first place. If he hadn't been so proud, he would never have killed the man he encountered in the road, his mother would never have been widowed, and the prophecy would never have come true. But there's also something a little unfair about it all, since Greeks believed that it was all predestined anyway: Oedipus would end up fulfilling the prophecy whether he liked it or not. The main 'moral' of Greek tragedy, then, seems to be: life isn't fair. Those goats sang for nothing.

# ⬦ Satyrical ⬦

We all know about tragedy and comedy, and these both have their origins in Greek theatre. But there was also an obscure third genre of drama: the satyr play.

The satyr play was a bawdy satire or burlesque which featured actors sporting large strap-on penises – the phallus being a popular symbol of fertility and virility, linked with the god Dionysus. Although satyr plays were often satirical in tone, there is no connection between 'satyr' and 'satire': the genre derives its name from the mythical beast, half-man, half-goat, which featured in such plays.

Euripides, Sophocles and Aeschylus – the three great tragedians of Greek theatre – all lived and worked shortly after the earliest record of the satyr play, in around 500 BCE, although some primitive form of the satyr play may have been performed much earlier. So it may be the case that comedy and tragedy even developed *from* the satyr play, or at least its prototype.

A satyr play tended to use stories from Greek myth and then subvert or parody them. The short plays would feature a chorus of satyrs – goat–man hybrids. At the City Dionysia, the festival at which plays would be performed, a playwright would put forward a trilogy of tragic plays followed by a satyr play as the finale. One playwright would then be proclaimed the winner of the festival. The whole festival was dedicated to Dionysus but, as mentioned, this tradition probably grew out of earlier religious rituals pertaining to crops, fertility and rebirth.

Only one satyr play survives in its entirety: written by the great tragedian Euripides, *Cyclops* centres on the incident from the story of Odysseus when the Greek hero found himself a prisoner in the cave of Polyphemus, the one-eyed monster (I won't make a phallus joke here). After *Cyclops*, the next-best-preserved satyr play is *Ichneutae* ('trackers') by Sophocles.

This idea of ending a trilogy of high tragedies – works of considerable emotive power – with a short piece of comic burlesque seems odd to us. But in fact the practice survived, in only slightly altered form, into Shakespeare's time: the Bard's tragedies would originally be followed by a short 'jig' in the Elizabethan theatres, a little skit or comic sketch which would round off the afternoon's entertainment for the audience – following Romeo and Juliet's tragic deaths or Macbeth's bloody end.

## ✦ The Roman Gatsby ✦

Three of the most important works of Western literature from the 1920s, T. S. Eliot's *The Waste Land*, James Joyce's *Ulysses*, and F. Scott Fitzgerald's *The Great Gatsby*, all tip a wink to a remarkable work of literature from classical Rome that has survived only as fragments. Depending on your view, it's either one of the first novels ever written, or a scandalous piece of trashy pornography. Its title – the *Satyricon*, meaning 'satyr-like adventures' – provides a clue to the bawdiness on offer.

The book's author, Petronius, is equally curious. He was at the court of the Emperor Nero (where he held the rather splendid title *elegantiae arbiter* or 'Arbiter of Elegance') in the first century. The historian Tacitus reported that Nero thought nothing charming unless Petronius approved of it first. Unfortunately, this high opinion didn't last: Nero ended up thinking that the most charming thing Petronius could do was kill himself. It appears that a scheming rival named Tigellinus, jealous of Petronius' high standing, contrived to convince Nero that his trusty Arbiter of Elegance was a traitor. Nero eventually ordered his former favourite's death. Petronius chose to execute the sentence himself, opening up a vein in his wrists and allowing himself slowly to bleed to death while he nattered away to his friends about poetry and shared a light meal. Even his own death was turned into art.

> F. Scott Fitzgerald initially toyed with calling *The Great Gatsby* 'Trimalchio in West Egg', drawing a parallel between the rich party-thrower Jay Gatsby and the affluent host in Petronius' masterpiece.

The title of his novel, the *Satyricon*, carries a double meaning: it refers to the bawdy satyrs of Greek myth (they of the giant strap-on penises), but it also suggests the book's satirical flavour. Specifically, the *Satyricon* is Menippean satire (a form of satire which mocks general attitudes rather than specific individuals or institutions), a sprawling melange of drunkenness, debauchery, heated discussions about art and education, and visits to the lavatory. The portion of the book that has survived – probably something like less than a tenth of the entire work, and perhaps far less – follows the book's narrator, a former gladiator named Encolpius, and his lover, a teenage servant-boy called Giton. Much of this surviving fragment focuses on the lavish feast put on by Trimalchio, an obscenely wealthy former slave.

Is the *Satyricon* great art or lurid pornography? That interminable debate about literary works begins, in many ways, with Petronius' novel – indeed, if it can even be called a 'novel'. It's certainly remarkably modern in all sorts of ways, not least for its focus on the real, everyday lives of Roman people (before Petronius, classical poetry and drama tended to depict human beings idealistically rather than realistically). As Steven Moore notes in *The Novel: An Alternative History*, Petronius' book shares much with James Joyce's modern masterpiece *Ulysses*: the loose reworking of the plot of Homer's *Odyssey*, the scurrilous obscenity, the diversity of literary style and the engagement with previous works of literature. But Petronius was writing nearly two millennia before Joyce, whose *Ulysses* was published in 1922. T. S. Eliot's poem *The Waste Land*, also published in 1922, takes its epigraph from Petronius' work.

Petronius' novel is one of the first-ever narratives in which the narrator is also one of the characters in the story, rather than the general detached narrator of the romances and epics produced up until this time. For this and myriad other reasons it represents a decisive moment in the development of fiction.

## ✧ True Story . . . ✧

Pinpointing the starting point of science fiction is a tricky undertaking. Did it all begin with Jules Verne's *Journey to the Centre of the Earth* in 1864? Or Mary Shelley's *Frankenstein* in 1818? Some notable authors in the genre, among them Isaac Asimov and Carl Sagan, give the mantle to the astronomer Johannes Kepler, whose *Somnium*, written in Latin in 1608, speculated on what the Earth might look like from the moon. (Like Asimov and Sagan, Kepler, it would seem, was both a scientist *and* a writer of science fiction.) But the origins of science fiction can be traced back far earlier even than Kepler.

Indeed, we have to go right the way back to the second century CE and to a Syrian writer named Lucian, whose short work *A True History* has a claim to being the first-ever work of science fiction. Lucian was born in what is modern-day Turkey, spent much of his adult life in Syria, spoke Greek, and lived under the Roman

Empire. He was a satirist who wrote in a variety of genres, and one of the genres he played around with was the prose romance – what would later be given the name of 'novel'. In fact, Lucian arguably represents the starting-point of both science fiction and the comic dialogue, which later practitioners such as Oscar Wilde would make their own. Another of his works, *Philopseudes* ('lover of lies'), is the source of the 'Sorcerer's Apprentice' story later made famous by Goethe and the composer Paul Dukas, among others.

*A True History* is essentially a parody of the far-fetched travel writings of antiquity: classical explorers who never let the truth get in the way of a good story. Fantastical places and improbable events were often reported as true in travel accounts of the time; Lucian wittily turns this on its head by admitting up front that his story is a lie from start to finish. Because his intention is to poke fun at the incredible claims made by other writers, Lucian's imagination is allowed a free rein: in his story we encounter rivers flowing with wine and islands made of cheese, as well as trees that are grown from men's testicles and develop into the shape of penises.

The actual story of *A True History* similarly requires not so much a suspension of disbelief as a full-on levitation act. The narrator's ship is blown out of the Mediterranean by a gigantic whirlwind and cast up into outer space (thus becoming the first spaceship, we might say). It eventually lands on the moon, whose king is at war with the king of the sun over the colonization of Venus. The lunar army features giant spiders bigger than the Cyclades, which spin webs between the moon and Venus to act as a sort of gossamer battlefield, while the solar army includes ants over two hundred feet long, giant mosquitoes, and an army of 'Sky-Dancers' whose main weaponry consists of large radishes that they hurl at the enemy, causing them to collapse and die of a malodorous but unspecified wound.

Lucian is, as you'd expect, a bit hazy on the detail as to how his narrator gets to the moon: a powerful whirlwind seems to be the sole method of propulsion. But the book certainly sowed the seeds for later works of bona fide science fiction, from Jules Verne's *From the Earth to the Moon* to H. G. Wells's *The First Men in the Moon* and beyond. And because it uses a fantastical narrative to satirize contemporary literary trends, it is also the precursor to later works such as Thomas More's *Utopia* and *Gulliver's Travels* by Jonathan Swift.

## ⊹ Pliny's History ⊹

When Vesuvius erupted in 79 CE, it laid waste to three large Italian settlements. Pompeii is the one everyone knows about, but the towns of Herculaneum and Oplontis were also engulfed. One of the many casualties during the eruption was the philosopher and naturalist Pliny the Elder.

It is often said that Pliny perished in the Vesuvian eruption because of his burning curiosity. Intrigued by the smoke coming out of the volcano, the story goes, he foolishly went to take a closer look. It's a nice story – the curious philosopher whose curiosity cost him his life – but the truth (or at least the account offered by Pliny's own nephew of his uncle's death) is a little different. After the destruction of Pompeii and Herculaneum had already occurred, Pliny sailed to the nearby town of Stabiae in order to help rescue a close friend, Pomponianus. Having arrived, Pliny discovered that the wind was against them and a swift getaway was impossible, so he did the only thing he could do in the circumstances: he ran a bath. The building in which they were sheltering threatened to collapse on them, so the party had to flee, taking their chances with the fragments of lava that were now showering down on the town. It was while trying to escape that Pliny, who was asthmatic, fell down and died. The image of him walking up to Vesuvius to take a closer look, with a pillow tied to his head with a strip of linen, is untrue – though Pliny and his crew did use pillows to protect themselves from the raining lava as they made their way to Stabiae.

Still, one can see how the story of his death came to be mythologized, since there was perhaps no Roman writer more curious than Pliny. Gaius Plinius Secundus (23–79 CE) is thought to have written some seventy-five books and kept a staggering 160 notebooks. He was, without doubt, a workaholic: he had a day job as an administrator for Vespasian, the Roman emperor, but he had a burning curiosity, a desire to examine just about everything around him, from emeralds (which could reportedly be used to cure leprosy) to hyena penis dipped in honey (used by women as a sexual fetish, apparently). He filled his numerous notebooks with his observations. But just one of his books is now widely known: *Natural History*. In this book Pliny gave himself the modest aim to 'set forth in detail all the contents of the entire world'. He read voraciously, declaring that no book was so bad that some good couldn't be got out of it. He was at work on *Natural History* – which by this time ran to thirty-seven volumes – when he died in the Vesuvius eruption.

What made Pliny's *Natural History* so influential on later works of science and history was its structure as much as its scope: containing an index as well as references to the original authors for relevant information, it would become a model for subsequent scholarly publications. It was also one of the first books to include a table of contents, an idea Pliny had picked up from the Roman poet and grammarian Quintus Valerius Soranus. *Natural History* has been called the first encyclopedia, but it's probably better to view it as an eye-opening – and occasionally jaw-dropping – window into Roman life and culture.

According to his nephew, Pliny the Younger, *Natural History* was largely written at night and during any free moments its author could grab when he wasn't on official business for Vespasian. This method of composition may account for some of the more outlandish theories (to put it politely) that found their way into the book. At one point, he describes people with dogs' heads instead of human heads as though they are real. He writes of people with no heads at all, and people with no mouths who eat through their nostrils. He also dutifully describes one-legged humans who use their solitary foot as a sunshade. Some of Pliny's book reads as not so much *Natural History* as *True History* – Lucian's, that is.

Then there are some of the cures and remedies, which practitioners of modern medicine would, quite frankly, find laughable. A headache could be cured by tying a fox's 'male organ' to the forehead, 'worn as an amulet'. Haemorrhoids could be treated either with a fresh root of rosemary (rubbed on the relevant area) or with a cream prepared from pig lard mixed with rust taken from a chariot's wheels. (Shoving an onion up your rectum also came highly recommended.) Garlic, meanwhile, was the cure-all: it could be used to treat just about everything from epilepsy to rheumatism, ulcers and, yes, haemorrhoids. Rubbing mouse droppings on a bald head would, Pliny assures us, restore a full head of hair. In 1469 *Natural History* became one of the first-ever classical texts to be printed. How many heads of hair were restored thanks to Pliny's advice has not, alas, been recorded.

## ✧ The Oldest Joke Book ✧

It's nearly the end of the chapter, so how about a joke? Have you heard the one about the idiot, the barber and the bald man who go camping? In order to ensure nobody makes off with their stuff as they sleep, they agree to take turns to stay up all night on watch, in four-hour shifts. The barber takes the first watch, and to amuse himself during his shift he takes out his razor and cuts the sleeping idiot's hair off. When the barber's four-hour stint is over, he wakes up the idiot to take over. The idiot, feeling his hairless head, exclaims: 'What a moron that barber is! He's woken up the bald bloke instead of me.'

This is an excerpt from the oldest surviving joke book, *Philogelos*. It may not have been the first-ever collection of jokes, but it's the oldest one that's come down to us – pretty intact, too. Some of the jokes still work, though they're as subject to the vagaries of individual taste as modern gags. One of them, involving a conversation between a slave-owner and a customer, has even been called the classical world's answer to Monty Python's 'Dead Parrot' sketch. A disgruntled customer goes to a slave-owner and complains that the slave the man sold him has gone and died. Shocked, the slave-owner replies, 'He never did anything like that when I owned him.' There's certainly a similarity, albeit of a superficial sort. But the crucial thing is that the structure of many of the jokes is strikingly familiar: their one-line or two-line narratives succinctly deliver a set-up and punchline in the manner of many modern comedians.

Its title translating roughly as 'the laughter-lover' or 'the joker', *Philogelos* was compiled by two Greek men, Hierokles and Philagrios, in around the third or fourth century, when Greece had become part of the Roman empire. It contains around 260 short jokes, many of which feature a particular kind of person. A fair number of the gags focus on a fool or idiot figure, though there are also jokes about – and, more specifically, at the expense of – various ethnic groups, which seems to mean anyone not fortunate enough to have been born Greek. These include the Kymaeans (known principally for being stupid), Sidonians (who are viewed as quite stupid), and Abderites (who, as well as being stupid, appear to have somehow attracted a reputation for getting hernias a lot).

But the best bits of *Philogelos* have much in common with our own style of humour. One of the best-known jokes involves an exchange between a barber and his customer. Asked how he would like his hair cut, the customer replies, 'In silence.' There's a quip about a man who is particularly tight with money, who, drawing up his will, names himself as the heir to his fortune; in another joke, one of a pair of identical twins dies, and a fool, meeting the surviving twin, asks him if it was him or his brother who died. Other jokes are at the expense of women, or, more specifically, wives: in one, a man brags to his friend, 'I slept with your wife last night.' The friend retorts, 'As her husband I *have* to; but what's your excuse?' People who remarked that the material used by many 1970s comedians was not so fresh were clearly right.

Certainly, if nothing else, *Philogelos* proves that the ancients had a sense of humour not all that different from our own. How funny they were remains a moot point. One Greek Stoic philosopher, Chrysippus of Soli, reportedly laughed so hard at his own joke (about a donkey drinking wine to wash down some figs it had gorged on) that he dropped down dead. One suspects you had to be there. Still, it was said of Isaac Newton that he was only known to have laughed once in his entire life, and that was when somebody asked him what was the point of studying Euclid. Which lends a new meaning to the phrase 'the elements of comedy'.

# THE MIDDLE AGES

It's not easy to determine who owned the largest library in medieval England, but a man named Richard de Bury would have to be a contender. A fourteenth-century bishop of Durham, de Bury appears to have been something of an incurable bibliophile whose private library dwarfed those of his fellow bishops. His rooms were so chock-full of books that visitors often had difficulty finding somewhere to sit down. It's little wonder that he's been described by his biographer Samuel Lane Boardman as the patron saint of book-lovers. Whether you're a bibliophile, a bibliomaniac, a bibliognost (one who knows books), a bibliophagist (a devourer of books), or a bibliosmiac (a book-sniffer), you'd probably have got on with Richard de Bury.

De Bury even wrote a book about his book obsession, *Philobiblon* (literally, 'love of books'), which has been described as the first-ever book about library management. In it he outlined why he loved books and why it was important to take care of them. He completed it shortly before his death in 1345.

As we will learn in this chapter, sometimes books have survived because the right person has come along to discover them, or save them from oblivion. The Middle Ages – roughly extending from the fall of Rome in the fifth century to the beginning of the Renaissance around a thousand years later – were precarious times. Life could be cheap, disease was everywhere, and war was a part of life. Three years after the good bishop joined the great library in the sky, the Black Death would arrive in England, killing a third of the population. In an age in which people had difficulty surviving from one year to the next, it's little wonder that books should have had trouble keeping themselves in existence. But many did – and it is the textual treasures of the medieval age that this chapter will examine.

## ⟡ Anglo-Saxon Attitudes ⟡

Although it is celebrated nowadays as an important work of Anglo-Saxon – indeed, 'English' – literature, the great epic poem *Beowulf* was virtually unknown and forgotten about for nearly a thousand years.

The plot of *Beowulf* is fairly simple. Most people know that the poem records the struggle of the title character in vanquishing a monster named Grendel. But what is less well known is that Beowulf has to slay not one big monster, but three: after he has taken care of Grendel, the dead monster's mother shows up, and she proves even more of a challenge for our hero, although ultimately he triumphs and wins the day. The poem then ends with Beowulf, now in his twilight years, slaying a third monster (this time, a dragon), although this encounter proves his undoing, as he is fatally wounded in the battle. The poem ends with his subsequent death and 'burial' at sea. Nobody's sure when the poem was composed, but it was written down in around the year 1000.

Although it is often thought of as the first great work of English literature (and often taught on English Literature courses as such), *Beowulf*, in many ways, has little to do with England. It is a tale about Scandinavians, set in Denmark, and told by Germans (the Angles from north-west Germany), although it was written in England after the Angles' and Saxons' invasion (they first began to settle in Britain from the fifth century). The poem may have been written in England, but the notion of 'Englishness' was at this time still taking shape, and the poem is heavily indebted to Germanic heroic poetry rooted in an oral tradition that pre-dated the arrival of the Angles and Saxons in Britain, although whether the specific tale of Beowulf pre-dated the written version of the poem, nobody knows for sure. But then again, since the word 'English' stems from the very Germanic peoples – the Angles – who brought the idea of *Beowulf* to Britain in the first place, perhaps it might be more appropriate to see *Beowulf* as the *most* 'English' work of literature there is.

Yet after the Norman Conquest in 1066, *Beowulf* seems to disappear from view. The poem was only rescued from obscurity in 1815, when someone decided it might be an idea to print an edition of it. But in fact in many ways it's nothing short of a miracle that we have the poem at all. That we can read it in modern times, whether in the original translation or in some translation such as that undertaken by Seamus Heaney, is largely down to two men, an Icelandic–Danish scholar named G. J. Thorkelin and an obscure English MP and antiquarian by the name of Sir Robert Cotton.

*Beowulf* only survived in one manuscript until the nineteenth century, when it was eventually copied down. Prior to that, there was one version in existence in the whole world, and it was by chance that this copy landed in Cotton's hands. In fact, all of the Anglo-Saxon poetry we have, we have because of *four* manuscripts that survived: the Cotton manuscript (which includes *Beowulf*), the Exeter Book, the Vercelli book, and the manuscripts of the Bodleian Library at Oxford.

Despite Cotton's preservation of the manuscript of the poem, the world seems to have been reluctant to do anything with *Beowulf* immediately. Instead, after Cotton's death, it was moved from place to place and, much like Beowulf himself in the poem, seems to have lurched from one narrow scrape with disaster to another: it managed to escape being destroyed during the Civil War of the 1640s (largely thanks to the efforts of an antiquarian who had taken up Cotton's mantle), only to be badly damaged in a fire in 1731, along with the rest of Cotton's collection.

*Beowulf* survived, dog-eared but intact, into the early nineteenth century when Thorkelin entered the scene. Thorkelin hired somebody from the British Museum to make a copy of the poem, working from Cotton's manuscript. He then set about preparing a modern translation – the first of many to be undertaken – only for the Battle of Copenhagen of 1807 to put paid to his efforts. During the conflict the scholar's house was burned down and the manuscript – the work of some twenty years transcribing 3,182 lines of poetry – was destroyed.

However, Thorkelin managed to salvage from the wreckage of his house the transcription of the original poem, and set to work on his translation again, publishing it – finally – in 1815. It was a timely publication: within the ensuing decades, Cotton's manuscript of the poem would deteriorate to the point where many parts of the text would become illegible, so we have Thorkelin and his translation to thank for the fact that we have a full, intact *Beowulf* to read at all.

Ten years after the publication of Thorkelin's translation, the first university course in Old English was introduced at the University of Virginia, in 1825. It would be nearly another hundred years before Oxford and Cambridge introduced English Literature courses. When they did so, *Beowulf* headed the university curriculum: at Oxford, none other than J. R. R. Tolkien lectured on the poem for many years. Now it is hard to imagine the story of English literature without *Beowulf*, but the poem has only attracted the attention it deserves in the last century or two. And it's all thanks to a curious MP and a persistent scholar.

## ✦ Merlin's Debut ✦

The stories of King Arthur draw upon a similar historical time period to *Beowulf*. Indeed, both names, Arthur and Beowulf, are thought by some linguists to have etymological connections with bears, conveying their fearsome might and dauntless courage (though in both cases the theory has been disputed). The chief difference is that Arthur fought against the Angles and Saxons, the very people who brought the tale of Beowulf with them to Britain. Arthur is a pre-Saxon figure, king of the 'Britons' or natives, defending his land against the Germanic hordes.

Arthur's story has been told countless times by writers down the ages, since at least the ninth century. As a result, there are some strange and inconsistent ideas surrounding the legend. Most people know of the tale of the 'sword in the stone' – memorably told, or rather retold, by T. H. White in his 1938 novel *The Sword in the Stone*, later filmed by Disney – which features Arthur plucking Excalibur from a stone, an act that could only be performed by the true king. (This myth may have its basis in the very real practice of casting metal swords in stone moulds, from which they would have to be extracted once the metal had set.) But in most renderings of the tale, the sword Arthur pulls from the stone is not Excalibur: Excalibur is the sword he receives later, once he has been crowned king, from the Lady of the Lake. In some versions of the story, it is Galahad who has to pull the sword from the stone. In others, Bedivere, not Arthur, receives the sword from the Lady of the Lake. In the earliest romances, it is Arthur's nephew Gawain who owns a sword named Excalibur. These inconsistencies are a result of the fact that many authors, not one, have contributed to the Arthurian story, so there is no definitive version of the legend. Instead, our idea of Arthuriana is an amalgamation and conflation of various myths, stories and rewritings.

However, if there was one writer who helped to bring Arthur to an international audience, it was the twelfth-century Welsh cleric Geoffrey of Monmouth, whose *Historia Regum Britanniae* or *History of the Kings of Britain* was the most influential text for later writers of the Arthur myth. Geoffrey's *History* was a medieval bestseller in a world before printed books. As we've seen, *Beowulf* survived in one single scorched manuscript; there are over 200 copies of Geoffrey's *History* from the medieval period. When Geoffrey was writing, the line between history and fiction was by no means easy to draw, and as a result we cannot say how much of his *History* is grounded in fact and how much was later invention, whether his own or other people's.

> The nineteenth-century French scholar Gaston Paris suggested that Geoffrey changed the Welsh *Myrddin* to Merlin to avoid resemblance to the Latin *merda*, 'faeces'.

Geoffrey's account of the legendary king contains the first appearance of many of the iconic features of the Arthurian myth, including the wizard Merlin. (It also features some strange notions, such as the theory that Merlin was responsible for the construction of Stonehenge, having taken the huge stones from Ireland by magic. People remained confused about Stonehenge for some time after this: the seventeenth-century architect Inigo Jones thought it was a Roman monument.) As if all this wasn't enough of a cultural legacy, Geoffrey's *History* is also ultimately the source (albeit indirectly) for two of Shakespeare's plays, *King Lear* and *Cymbeline*.

Geoffrey of Monmouth had his own agenda in popularizing the Arthur myth, though quite what that agenda was continues to divide critics. He could well have been suggesting that the arrival of the Normans at the Battle of Hastings had put an end to the squabbles between the Saxons and the native Britons such as Arthur, but if this is the case, it's somewhat ironic that Geoffrey himself was writing against the backdrop of a bloody civil war raging between the Norman king Stephen and his cousin, Empress Matilda. What is certain is that subsequent authors have also reworked the Arthurian tale to reflect their own times. Francis of Assisi remarked that Arthur, along with other medieval pin-ups such as Charlemagne and Roland, were Christian martyrs who had been prepared to die in battle to defend their faith in Christ. There were numerous retellings of the Arthur legend throughout the Middle Ages, such as that by the Norman author Wace (pronounced 'wassy'), who added the Round Table, the French writer Chrétien de Troyes' poems of the late twelfth century (which added the character of Lancelot and the adulterous affair with Guinevere, wife of Arthur), the *Alliterative Morte Arthure* written in Middle English and dating from around 1400, and – most enduringly of all – Sir Thomas Malory's fifteenth-century prose work *Le Morte d'Arthur*.

## ⟡ Before Marco Polo ⟡

In the prologue to his *Travels*, the Venetian explorer Marco Polo claims to have travelled more extensively than anyone before him; remarkably, this is probably no exaggeration. But he was not, as is widely thought, the first European to travel to the Far East and write about it. That honour goes to a fellow Italian who died two years before Polo was even born, named Giovanni da Pian del Carpine and often known in English as John of Plano Carpini.

Carpini, a Franciscan monk and former disciple of the more famous St Francis of Assisi, was an old man and reportedly rather fat when he undertook his voyage to the Far East, where he was granted an audience with the Great Khan, Kuyuk (grandson of

Genghis). Quite what he was doing there has been the topic of much speculation, but it's probable that he was on a spy mission, given the particular interest in the Mongols' military strategies which his book displays. But he also gives us a valuable insight into the Mongols' marriage practices, the food they ate, the clothing they wore, their laws and customs, and much else. He wrote up his report of his travels in the late 1240s, and became something of a celebrity in his final years, as the man who had first revealed the Mongol world to European Christians.

It would be another fifty years before Marco Polo would get round to writing up *his* travels. What's more, the Mongolia that Polo visited was the home of an empire in decline; Carpini visited it when it was still a great power. Carpini's account also has the ring of truth, something that cannot always be said of Polo's *Travels*. (Polo didn't help himself by mistaking rhinoceroses for unicorns, and whimsically placing himself in the midst of battles and other key events which he almost certainly wasn't around to witness.) In 1995, Frances Wood even wrote a book titled *Did Marco Polo Go to China?* The answer, Wood concludes, is 'No'. Wood is doubtful that Polo ever got beyond the Black Sea. Other scholars, however, disagree and think that, while some of his claims were undoubtedly exaggerated, Polo was speaking from first-hand experience of 'Cathay', as China was known at the time.

This is not to deny the enormous popularity that Polo enjoyed, or the influence his *Travels* had. His book, dictated by Polo to a fellow prisoner in around 1300, is an account of his travels around the Middle East and the Far East, from Armenia to Indonesia and virtually everywhere, or so it seems, in between. He shares with us his brushes with the great and not-so-good (most famously Kubla Khan, grandson of Genghis), and even his bouts of diarrhoea through drinking the 'green' and brackish water in the Iranian desert. (One drop of it, he tells us in words that have the ring of experience, is enough to make you void your bowels ten times over.) The *Travels* also provided the West with a host of indispensable new inventions: Polo's book is credited with introducing both paper money and spectacles to Europe. Columbus took the book on his famous voyage of 1492.

But it is worth bearing in mind that Carpini was there before Polo, and it is to him that the honour of 'first Westerner to write a popular book about the Far East' should go.

## ✧ Flatulent Demons ✧

The poet Dante Alighieri was a contemporary of Marco Polo, though one finds it hard to imagine them knocking about together. Dante's travels were geographically less ambitious but theologically far more extensive than Polo's. He is best-remembered for the epic poem about heaven, hell, damnation, purgatory and salvation called *The Divine Comedy*, though that title was unknown in Dante's own lifetime. It wasn't named *The Divine Comedy* by Dante himself, who referred to it simply as the *Commedia*. His fellow Italian poet Boccaccio called it the *Divina*, but it wasn't given the title *Divina Commedia* until 1555, two and a half centuries after it was written.

It's not a 'comedy' because it's funny — readers looking for belly laughs will come away disappointed — but essentially because it's *not* a tragedy written in the high language of Latin. Instead, it's about journeying from hell to paradise — somewhat more upbeat than your average tragedy – and it's composed in the Italian vernacular of the day. Dante's journey begins on Good Friday 1300 (about the same time Marco Polo was busy dictating his travels in prison) during Dante's thirty-fifth year, halfway through his biblical threescore and ten. It might be viewed as the original fantasy trilogy, charting the poet's journey from hell to purgatory before arriving in heaven, 'Paradiso'. It's certainly the first great work of Italian literature to have been written *in* Italian rather than Latin.

T. S. Eliot, to whom Dante meant a great deal, said of Dante's work that genuine poetry is able to communicate before it is fully understood. Nevertheless, Dante is undoubtedly more known about than he is avidly read these days. Voltaire wrote of Dante in 1764: 'His reputation will go on increasing, because scarce anybody reads him.' Those who make the attempt may be put off by the unusual and repetitive verse form employed – *terza rima*, a three-line stanza structure – or by the references to figures from Italian medieval history who now mean little or nothing to us. (One notable exception is the Montagues and Capulets: Shakespeare's rival families from *Romeo and Juliet* had their origins in historical fact, it would seem.)

It doesn't help, either, that theology, as a topic for poetry, is not the exciting draw that it once was. But it would be wrong to think that Dante's poetry is all abstract religious doctrine and vague talk of sin and redemption. It's a surprisingly visual and often visceral work, much of it preoccupied with the body as much as the soul. In her book *On Farting: Language and Laughter in the Middle Ages*, Valerie Allen discusses the more flatulent moments in Dante's religious epic. Malacoda, one of the demons who helps Dante and his trusty guide, the Roman poet Virgil, to negotiate the various circles of Hell, makes a trumpet of his backside and farts at his fellow demons. Elsewhere, Dante provides an image of sinners being cooked in a giant sewer of food, filth and farts. And there's more. At one point in the *Inferno*, the poet sees a host of tormented sufferers covered in diarrhoea that appears to be flowing out of cubicles, as if hell has become a giant public toilet.

Such lavatorial descriptions are not meant to be fun, as they are in, say, the *Satyricon*. Dante's purpose in writing *The Divine Comedy* was partly political: at the time, the city of Florence had been taken over by a faction known as the 'Blacks', Dante's political enemy: Dante himself belonged to the rival 'Whites'. The Whites resisted papal control, arguing for a greater degree of autonomy within Florence, while the Blacks gave the Pope more power within the city state. Dante, as a prominent mover and shaker among the Whites, was banished from Florence by the Blacks on pain of death: he was told he would be burned at the stake if he was seen in the city again.

> Rumour has it that Dante taught his cat to hold a candle up for him in its paw while he was eating or reading.

The most famous things about the poem are probably the various circles of hell that Dante describes, and the young girl, Beatrice, to whom Dante was devoted, despite only ever meeting her twice. To modern minds Dante's admiration for Beatrice may sound odd, but Dante, who had first clapped eyes on Beatrice when he himself was but a boy, viewed her as a paragon of purity and virtue, revering her almost as a goddess on Earth. When Beatrice died in her twenties in 1290, Dante wrote his first major work, a mixture of poetry and prose called *La Vita Nuova* ('The New Life'), as a tribute to her. It is Beatrice who reveals the world of heaven to Dante in the final part of the *Comedy*. As for the circles of hell, there are nine in total, many of them taking one of the seven deadly sins as their focus. In the ninth circle, associated with treachery, Satan sits right in the centre of hell, up to his waist in ice (it's not all fire and brimstone in Dante's vision of the inferno) and sporting three faces – one black, one blood-red, and one pale yellow. It would seem that where the Devil is concerned, being *two*-faced isn't quite treacherous enough.

His fellow Italian writer Boccaccio records that, when Dante's mother was pregnant with him, she dreamt that he transformed into a peacock. In the end, all he managed to become was Italy's first great poet of the post-classical era. Which, while less impressive as a feat of metamorphosis, is nevertheless a resounding achievement.

## ☽ Chaucer's Astronomy ☽

In the early 1370s, a young Geoffrey Chaucer travelled to Italy on a diplomatic mission for King Edward III. While he was there he also found time to familiarize himself with the fruits of what can only be described as a golden age of Italian literature: the sonnets of Petrarch, the work of Boccaccio (whose *Decameron*, featuring a group of people telling stories, would serve as the model for Chaucer's own *Canterbury Tales*), and Dante.

Like Dante before him, Chaucer wrote more besides the one big book he is principally known for. As well as *The Canterbury Tales*, there's *Troilus and Criseyde*, telling the story of the star-crossed couple from the Trojan Wars, and 'An ABC', one of his earliest works, an acrostic poem for people to use in prayer. Like much of Chaucer's work, 'An ABC' was a Middle English translation of a French work, in this case a prayer written by Guillaume de Deguileville. Each of the twenty-six eight-line stanzas begins with a successive letter of the alphabet. Probably written in the 1370s, the poem shows Chaucer's art in its early stages of development. (Chaucer had been born in London around 1343 – the precise date of his birth is not known. His surname, by the way, derives from the French *chausseur*, 'shoemaker'.)

Chaucer also wrote an early work of popular science: his *Treatise on the Astrolabe* is possibly the first science book written in English, dating from around 1391. It is also one of the first books in English written for children: it was written for Chaucer's own son, Lewis.

An astrolabe (literally, 'star-taker') was an astronomical instrument used for a variety of purposes, but chiefly to calculate the position of stars in relation to the user's latitude on Earth. As a scientific instrument it would later be superseded by the sextant. We're in the realm of astrology as much as astronomy here: part of the astrolabe's purpose was to determine the movement of the zodiac so one could plot the orbits and positions of stars and planets in order to divine mystical meanings from them. But it was also a useful device for charting the astronomical calendar – in a sense, for plotting space and time. Chaucer's book is essentially an instruction manual, directing the reader in how to use the device and explaining what it is used for. It's a work of popular science because Chaucer is no expert astronomer, but an amateur enthusiast tinkering with the device, and encouraging his son to do so too.

Chaucer died in 1400; the date on his tomb in Westminster Abbey reads 25 October. He became the first person to be buried in Poets' Corner, though it was bureaucratic service rather than poetic achievement that earned Chaucer his place in the Abbey.

# ✧ A Medieval Cookbook ✧

We have Richard II to thank for several things. As well as providing Shakespeare with the subject for one of his finest early history plays, he is credited with introducing the handkerchief to England. He is also remembered for putting down the Peasants' Revolt while he was a boy of just fourteen.

But there is another thing for which we have Richard – in many ways a rather unpleasant king – to thank: the first cookbook written in English was compiled for him. *The Forme of Cury* ('the form of cooking') was put together by an anonymous author in around 1390. It contains nearly 200 recipes, including an early quiche (known then as a 'custard') and a 'blank mang', a sweet dish made with milk, rice, almonds, sugar and – er, slices of meat. It may not sound much but it was a popular dish at the time and would later evolve, for good or ill, into blancmange.

A number of ingredients – spices, in particular – feature in *The Forme of Cury*, making their debut in English records. Cloves and mace appear here for the first time in English cookery, and numerous other rare spices such as ginger, pepper and nutmeg are to be found in the recipes. Perhaps surprisingly – given that it is England's only native spice – mustard gets only one mention in the entire book, where it appears as 'mustard balls'.

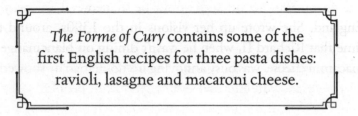

The *Forme of Cury* contains some of the first English recipes for three pasta dishes: ravioli, lasagne and macaroni cheese.

*The Forme of Cury* is also the first English book to mention olive oil. An early salad recipe is listed: it includes parsley, sage, rosemary, garlic, mint, shallots, onions, fennel, and other herbs and vegetables, all shredded together in oil, vinegar and salt (indeed, the word *salad* derives from the Latin for 'salted'). Many of the recipes in *The Forme of Cury* haven't lasted. But the book did have one enduring legacy. That word 'cury', Middle English for 'cookery', would continue to be used by English traders travelling to the Far East, and would eventually be applied – at least according to one theory – to the spicy sauces used in Asian cooking. Which, so many language historians believe, is how we got the word 'curry'.

## ⊹ A Woman's Revelations ⊹

On 8 May 1373, a thirty-year-old woman fell seriously ill – so ill that she nearly died. Deep in delirium, she experienced a series of visions – or 'shewings' as she herself called them – which she took to be revelations from God. Her name was Julian of Norwich – well, actually, it probably wasn't. Julian almost certainly wasn't her real name, but the name of the local church in the parish where she lived. But she would become known by that name and would be a medieval celebrity in England. She wrote up her visions in the 1390s, around the time that Richard II, when he wasn't dining on blancmange or macaroni cheese, was busy annoying his noblemen by showering his favourites with gifts and seizing land from people.

In the book outlining the nature of her delirious visions, Julian describes herself as 'unlettered', which has been taken as false modesty (clearly she was highly gifted to be able to write such a book) but which also points up the fact that she had not received the kind of thorough education normally reserved for privileged men at the time. It is for this reason that Julian did not write about her visions in Latin – the usual language for such books of the day – but English. *Revelations of Divine Love* thus became the first book written by a woman in the English language. Formal education's loss was the English language's gain.

Julian uses the Middle English of her day to describe and explore the series of sixteen visions which convinced her to become an anchorite and shut herself away from society, living in a nun's cell at her church in Norwich. Much of *Revelations* may seem incomprehensible to the non-religious mind, steeped as it is in theological contemplation of the visions she has experienced. Was it mere delirium, or divine communication? Most of the visions feature Jesus Christ, with a particular focus on the Crucifixion and Resurrection – though some of the most memorable accounts involve moments of great simplicity: at one point Christ comes to her and shows her a hazelnut containing 'all that is made'.

But for the majority of modern readers the most noteworthy thing about her book is not what she writes but how she writes. Because she was a woman she could not use the Latin reserved for the monks and professional theologians. But that is to her, and her book's, advantage. Hers is a democratic book, a book about ordinary English people, reflecting their experience of Christianity in their own language. (This is all somewhat ironic given that Julian shut herself away from everyone else.)

The most famous line from *Revelations of Divine Love* runs: 'Sin is behovely, but all shall be well, and all shall be well, and all manner of thing shall be well.' This is the real message of *Revelations*. Given that Julian's lifetime had seen the arrival of the Black Death in England, which had killed around a third of the population, and that she would live to see civil unrest (the Peasants' Revolt of 1381, for one), this was a timely message of comfort for a fraught period of English history. It is fitting that T. S. Eliot, when completing his *Four Quartets* in the midst of the Second World War in 1942, would choose to allude to Julian's message that 'all shall be well' in his poem of war and salvation, 'Little Gidding'.

## ⚶ The First Autobiography ⚶

In 1934, a man named William Erdeswick made a startling discovery. It was the kind that most literary scholars dream of, but Erdeswick was a lieutenant-colonel rather than a professor. In a cupboard in his house in Chesterfield, he found a copy of a manuscript that had been thought lost for five hundred years: the sole surviving copy of a book first transcribed in the 1430s and, as was later realized, the first work of autobiography ever written in the English language.

The author of the book, Margery Kempe, was a medieval pilgrim and mystic who, like Julian of Norwich a few decades before, had experienced vivid and powerful divine visions. A few years before the end of her life, the author of *Revelations of Divine Love* even received the middle-aged Kempe as a visitor to her cell in Norwich.

Although the book is often called the first English autobiography, Kempe tells 'her' story in the third person, using the term 'this creature' to refer to the central woman figure in the book – hardly the style of a deeply personal account. *The Book of Margery Kempe* is probably best viewed not as personal memoir but as a depiction of the typical lives of many Christian women during the period. Nevertheless, much of the book is related with a vivid clarity which smacks of personal experience that has then been universalized.

But a fair portion of her *Book* seems to revolve around trying to persuade her husband to keep his hands off her. Margery wished to be chaste because she was convinced that this was what the Lord expected of her. Her husband had other ideas, and presses her to allow him to enjoy his conjugal rights on virtually every page in the early sections of the book. Perhaps unsurprisingly, she ended up bearing him fourteen children. It was after the birth of her first child that she suffered the illness which led to her religious visions, and it was these visions that convinced her to devote her life to God. Unfortunately, her approach was deemed controversial for the time: she was accused of being a heretic, and threatened with being burned at the stake. Unlike Julian of Norwich before her, Margery was a wife and mother, and medieval mothers simply weren't supposed to do the things that Margery did. In fact, nobody was. She courted the wrong sort of attention wherever she went, weeping loudly throughout church services and performing odd acts of penance. On her way back from one of several pilgrimages – she travelled to both Jerusalem and Rome, as well as to other holy sites – she gave all her money away to the poor and was reduced to beggary, attracting unwanted attention from the authorities. Apparently, it's possible to follow Christ's lead *too* closely.

Her 'autobiography' (if we can so consider her *Book*) was dictated towards the end of a long and eventful life. Unlike Julian, Margery didn't write her account but dictated it: *The Book of Margery Kempe* was transcribed by an unknown writer in the 1430s. Extracts from it were published by the gloriously named early English printer Wynkyn de Worde in 1501, but much of it remained lost for centuries until Erdeswick made his extraordinary discovery. Now we can read the full thing, and whether we approach it as a powerful work of religious literature or as an account of one woman's life during the Middle Ages, it's a good thing that that manuscript turned up in Erdeswick's cupboard.

## ✤ Robin of Barnsdale ✤

Robin Hood makes his debut in writing in the late fourteenth-century poem *Piers Plowman*, which is commonly attributed to William Langland, a contemporary of Geoffrey Chaucer. It was a timely moment for the outlaw to enter literature:

English literature as we know it was starting to emerge, and the Peasants' Revolt – one leader of which, the priest John Ball, even quoted from Langland's poem – occurred in 1381, shortly after Robin Hood first appeared on the literary scene. It was a time when the social order of England was being challenged and feudalism was rapidly declining. The oldest surviving work of literature to detail Robin's adventures is the anonymous fifteenth-century ballad *A Gest of Robyn Hode*. The early printer Wynkyn de Worde helped to get some of the first Robin Hood tales into print, around fifty years later: by then, Robin Hood was well and truly part of the English literary landscape.

Friar Tuck, the famous man of the cloth among Robin's merry men, was a real person in fifteenth-century England, whose original name was Robert Stafford.

But where exactly *is* Robin's landscape? Why is Doncaster and Sheffield's airport named after Robin Hood, if the plucky outlaw lived in Nottinghamshire? There are several reasons. First, the earliest stories which mention Robin Hood are set in Yorkshire, not Nottinghamshire. Robin Hood's original home was Barnsdale Forest, not Sherwood (and in any case, the majority of the remaining woodland of Sherwood Forest is actually in Yorkshire, not Nottinghamshire). *A Gest*, for instance, makes no mention of Sherwood Forest. *A Gest* is, however, our source of many of the familiar features of the Robin Hood story, and many of the characters – Little John, Will Scarlet, Much the Miller's Son – first appeared in this anonymous poem. Robin Hood's cloak was scarlet in some of the Robin Hood tales: one nineteenth-century poem, for instance, has Robin in scarlet while his men don the famous Lincoln green.

Nottingham, while we're at it, derives its name from Snotingaham, the original name for the Saxon settlement that stood on the site of the present city: Snot was the Saxon chieftain who settled there, and somewhere along the way the initial 'S' was dropped.

In the original *Gest* story, Robin's king wasn't the absent, crusading Richard the Lionheart (reigned 1189–99) – *A Gest* refers to 'King Edward', not Richard or John, and this puts Robin Hood later in English history, some time after 1272 when Edward I ascended the throne.

The idea of Robin being an outlawed nobleman, Robin of Locksley, is far more recent: it derives from Sir Walter Scott's celebrated medieval romance *Ivanhoe* (1820). This novel has also been credited with helping to popularize medieval history for a generation of later writers and artists, among them Tennyson and the Pre-Raphaelites. More recently, Scott's novel provided the blockbuster 1991 movie starring Kevin Costner, *Robin Hood: Prince of Thieves*, with its source material for the character of Robin Hood (who is known throughout as 'Robin of Locksley'; Locksley, by the way, provides us with another Yorkshire connection, since Loxley is the name of a village and suburb of the city of Sheffield in South Yorkshire). Many people criticized Costner for playing Robin with an unashamedly American accent, but Alan Rickman himself appears to have remarked that the American accent was closer to twelfth-century Anglo-Saxon than modern British English is.

# THE RENAISSANCE

For the literary historian Stephen Greenblatt, it was a book that began the Renaissance. In *The Swerve: How the Renaissance Began*, Greenblatt argues that an Italian librarian's rediscovery in the fifteenth century of an all-but-forgotten classical text, Lucretius' epic poem *De Rerum Natura* ('On the Nature of Things'), sparked a resurgence of interest in long-abandoned theories of the universe, such as the notion that worldly events are governed by chance rather than divine will, and that everything is fundamentally composed of atoms. Granted, Lucretius also believed that worms spontaneously grew out of wet soil, and that winds in underground caves were responsible for earthquakes, but on the topic of atomic physics he was, in a startling way, correct.

The rediscovery of Lucretius' poem, Greenblatt argues, led to a 'swerve' away from Christian asceticism in favour of a focus on this world and the pleasures it can offer (Lucretius was a follower of Epicurus, who advocated the responsible pursuit of pleasure). Perhaps, though, things were not that simple. Reviewing Greenblatt's book, Robert Douglas-Fairhurst suggested that it was not one book, but rather the *invention* of the modern book itself, that gave the Renaissance its real momentum. Sure enough, Johannes Gutenberg's invention of movable type in the mid-fifteenth century, the technological innovation that made the printed book possible, allowed for a much freer and easier exchange of ideas across Europe and, in time, the entire Western world. Suddenly you didn't need a dozen monks slowly and slavishly copying out the Bible in their scriptorium: a printer in a workshop could produce hundreds of copies, for a fraction of the cost.

Eventually, among other things, this would enable people who would never have otherwise had ready access to the Bible – other than through the priest's Latin recital of it at mass – to scrutinize the word of God closely and carefully. Along with other factors, this would help to bring about the Christian Reformation, whereby Catholicism lost its claim to being the sole version of Christianity practised in much of the Western world. In fact, Catholicism hadn't had a true monopoly for some time: in England the Lollards, followers of John Wycliffe, had been active since the fourteenth century, rejecting many aspects of Roman Catholicism and advocating a return to a simpler form of worship. (Wycliffe was a near-contemporary of Chaucer, and undertook an English translation of much of the Bible – yet more evidence of this explosion of creativity among English writers during the fourteenth century.)

But the Lollards (the word comes from the Dutch for 'mumbler', from its practitioners' habit of muttering passages from the Bible) remained a relatively small group. It was the arrival of Protestantism in the sixteenth century that really gave Catholicism a run for its money, beginning on Halloween

1517 when the German monk Martin Luther nailed his ninety-five theses, or calls for religious reform, to the church door at Wittenberg. Within two decades, England had followed, with Henry VIII declaring himself the head of the Church of England – he, not the Pope, would be the religious leader of his country. Of course, Henry's motive was largely political: he wanted to get a divorce from his first wife, Catherine of Aragon, but the Pope refused to grant him permission. The upheaval and change wrought by Luther throughout Europe, and by Henry VIII in England, would exercise a profound effect on how people lived – and, as we'll see in this chapter, on the kinds of books people wrote.

Theoretically, the most expensive book in the world costs 153 million euros and is only 13 pages long. I say 'theoretically' because nobody has yet felt it was worth its somewhat inflated price. Called 'The Task', it's a short work by the self-proclaimed greatest philosopher of all time, Tomas Alexander Hartmann. Only one copy of his magnum opus will ever exist, Hartmann assures us, so to learn the answers to some of the world's biggest questions you need to have pretty deep pockets. As it stands, the most that anyone has ever actually *paid* for a single book is just under $31 million, when Bill Gates bought the *Codex Leicester*, better known as Leonardo da Vinci's notebooks. Few figures better exemplify the Renaissance than Leonardo, but it is with some altogether more everyday works – treating everything from bodily functions to Tudor attitudes towards cats – that this chapter is chiefly concerned. They won't cost you $31 million to acquire, but they are, in their own quiet ways, highly valuable artefacts.

# ✧ Gargantuan ✧

It takes a certain kind of writer to get their own adjective. Shakespearean, Dickensian, Orwellian: it helps if your work comes to typify, even define, a particular style or theme. Take *Rabelaisian*: pertaining to the writings of the French author François Rabelais (*c.*1494–1553), which are described by the *Oxford English Dictionary* as 'noted for their earthy humour, their parody of medieval learning and literature, and their affirmation of humanist values; bawdy, vulgar'. No other writer of the period did bawdy and vulgar quite like Rabelais.

Indeed, Rabelais, who wrote *Gargantua and Pantagruel*, gave us two popular adjectives, since one of his literary creations even inspired a word for something gigantic: *gargantuan*. The name Gargantua actually predates Rabelais (it first appeared in a book, *Great Chronicles of Gargantua*, published anonymously when Rabelais was still a boy), as does Pantagruel, which existed as Penthagruel, a little devil that preyed on drunkards. But Rabelais took these stock figures and put his indelible mark on them.

Rabelais also gave us the rather less famous word *panurgic*, denoting someone who is ready for anything, from the name of Pantagruel's sidekick, Panurge.

*Gargantua and Pantagruel*, as the complete book is often known, is actually a whopping four-parter, comprising the volumes *Pantagruel* (1532), *Gargantua* (1534), and the rather less originally titled *Third Book* (1546) and *Fourth Book* (1549; expanded 1552). This tetralogy of volumes (there was a fifth, though it's doubtful whether Rabelais wrote that) represents Rabelais' literary achievement.

Bawdiness – chiefly, nob and fart gags – is a big part of the Rabelaisian comedic fabric. Codpieces are discoursed upon at length. When Gargantua relieves himself, we are told that over a quarter of a million Parisians are drowned in his urine. Pantagruel, for his part, can produce 53,000 dwarves from his anus simply by letting out a colossal fart. But wine also splashes across nearly every page, as the names Gargantua (etymologically connected to 'gargle' and the throat) and Pantagruel ('all-thirsty') imply.

Voltaire dismissed Rabelais as a drunkard who wrote drunk; Balzac thought him the possessor of 'the greatest mind'. Which of them is right? Or are they both right? Rabelais has been variously seen as a great humorist, a rationalist, a writer of allegory, and even a great religious writer. But the image that Voltaire popularized of the wine-swigging Frenchman, glass in one hand and quill in the other, has endured, perhaps to the extent that the seriousness behind Rabelais' work has been obscured. True, Rabelais was undoubtedly a man of the people – a truly popular writer. But beneath the fart gags and sexual puns lies a serious intention: to expose hypocrisy. His day job was as a physician and a priest: from the first he picked up a detailed anatomical knowledge (which feeds into much of the physical humour in his writing), and from the second he learned the importance of moral responsibility and fairness, but also the hypocritical nature of many of his fellow humans. In *Gargantua*, one of the first prequels in literature (it was the second book Rabelais wrote, but is set before the first), we meet the Abbaye de Thélème, an 'anti-monastery' which allows in everyone except monks and hypocrites. The implication is that they're two sides of the same coin.

## ✧ The French *Decameron* ✧

In an abbey in the Pyrenees, ten people – five men and five women – take refuge from the dangerous world of bandits and wild bears beyond the abbey walls. To pass the time before it's safe to venture outside again, they agree to tell each other stories.

Such an idea – that of the framed narrative whereby a group of people sit around telling each other stories – was not exactly new when it was used as the framing device for the *Heptameron*, a curious sixteenth-century prose work attributed to Queen Marguerite of Navarre. Its title was a nod to the *Decameron*, the work of the fourteenth-century Italian prose writer Boccaccio, whose characters tell stories while they are holed up in a villa outside Florence, waiting for the Black Death to abate so they can return to the city. Indeed, the title of *Heptameron* was only given to Marguerite's book retrospectively, to draw comparisons with Boccaccio's celebrated work and imply that it was the French equivalent. As the title of Boccaccio's book suggests, the ten characters each tell ten stories: a whopping hundred tales in all. Between them, the ten raconteurs in Marguerite's *Heptameron* tell a total of seventy-two stories. (The *Decameron*'s framed narrative structure had also influenced Chaucer, whose *The Canterbury Tales* takes up the motif of the storytelling competition.)

Marguerite was the sister of François, King of Navarre, and patron of her fellow writer Rabelais, who returned the compliment by dedicating the third volume of *Gargantua and Pantagruel* to her. The Dutch scholar Desiderius Erasmus wrote to her admiringly, praising the 'many gifts' God had bestowed upon her. However, we don't know for sure that Marguerite even wrote the *Heptameron*. The first edition, published nine years after her death, does not mention her name. But scholars generally agree that she was probably the author, and almost certainly the compiler, of many of the stories the book contains. Either way, the book gives a valuable insight into life at a French royal court in the early sixteenth century.

Many of the tales in the *Heptameron* turn on trickery of some kind. A great number of the early stories involve sexual trickery, with lecherous men trying to lead virtuous wives astray, or scheming husbands, keen to climb into bed with the maid, ending up by some skulduggery in bed with . . . their own wives. As with Rabelais, there are plenty of wily and lustful monks. What's more, there's a good dollop of sex – but also, occasionally, a dollop of something else. A number of the stories are, to use the technical term, scatological in theme (or, to use the non-technical term, full of shit). In one short tale, an apothecary's assistant picks up a large poo from the street, wraps it in paper, and sells it to a lawyer, having convinced him it's a sugar loaf that would make a fine dinner. In another short skit, a wealthy noblewoman is taken short while visiting a convent. Many of the mini-narratives contained within the *Heptameron* are concerned with the body first and the soul second. We've come a long way since the religious meditations of Margery Kempe and Julian of Norwich, that's for sure.

## ✦ Is This Utopia? ✦

Most people know Sir Thomas More (1478–1535) for two things. The first is for falling foul of Henry VIII when Henry divorced Catherine of Aragon and married Anne Boleyn, with More ending up with his head on the block. The second is for writing a book called *Utopia*, which gave its name to any imagined ideal society and, by association, to a literary genre. Most of us don't read the original, because More wrote the book in Latin – the first English translation would appear in 1551.

*Utopia* owes more than a passing debt to Lucian's *True History*, which we encountered in the first chapter. But rather than coming clean at the outset, as Lucian had done, and admitting that his narrative is a fiction, More went to some pains to create a degree of realism surrounding his story, using the device of the frame narrative to suggest that the island of Utopia was a real place, much like the newly discovered Americas. He may have tried too hard: the publisher's introduction to More's Latin epigrams of 1518 referred to 'a certain fathead' who said he didn't see why More should be so admired for *Utopia* when all he had done was write down what he'd been told by somebody else.

Thomas More's friend Erasmus edited *Utopia*, and it was published in Leuven in 1516.

Indeed, nobody can quite agree whether More is pulling the reader's leg in *Utopia* or sincerely offering a vision of a perfect world. There are, however, some clues that much of the book, if not the whole thing, is supposed to be satirical: it's hard to see the staunchly Roman Catholic More seriously advocating divorce by mutual consent, something that is encouraged in Utopia, nor is it likely that he was in favour of women priests, very much a feature of More's looking-glass island republic. Once we realize that the very word Utopia is a pun (both 'good place' and 'no place' – in other words 'too good to be true') it becomes evident that More is poking fun at the world's excessive idealists. This is also apparent when he presents us with Utopians who promote a proto-communist rejection of personal wealth, and believe the best way to encourage a contempt for riches is – why, to have chamber pots made of gold, of course.

But what is perhaps most surprising about More's *Utopia*, whether he meant it to be a serious representation of an ideal society or a satirical take on one, is that much of it appears to be more *dys*topian than utopian. Big Brother is very much watching everyone in More's imagined world: there's no personal liberty, that great human right that is placed under threat in virtually every modern dystopian novel from George Orwell's *Nineteen Eighty-Four* to Margaret Atwood's *The Handmaid's Tale*. Yet More doesn't seem to think this presents a problem. Sex before marriage is punished by compulsory celibacy for life. Adulterers are taken as slaves, and repeat offenders are executed. There is much that is nightmarish in Utopia, at least for modern readers.

What's more, although he gave the genre its name, More didn't invent the notion of the fictional utopia. Ideal societies had long been a fixture of writers from the classical era onwards, beginning with the 4,000-year-old *Epic of Gilgamesh* and its description of a world free from death, mourning, sickness and old age. Plato's *Republic* continued the idea, and some scholars have even interpreted Plato's book – like More's own – as satirical in intent.

## ✧ The Governor ✧

The name Thomas Elyot (*c.*1490–1546) is virtually unknown now except to scholars of Tudor history, but there are several reasons he is worth knowing about. Elyot was a true humanist in the mould of Erasmus and Thomas More, the latter of whom he counted among his friends. He championed the idea that women should be educated, laying out his argument in the 1540 work *The Defence of Good Women* (the idea being that learned wives could serve their husbands better, through being able to discuss intellectual ideas with them).

He was an important figure in the development of English prose, too. Many words still in common use are first recorded in Elyot's writing, including abusive, adapt, adult, boyish, concoction, encyclopedia, excrement, fragment, inimitable, involuntary, loyal, ode, perfume, ridiculous, spearmint, starfish, tension, tolerate and – rather splendidly – turnip. He also provides the first recorded use of the word 'alligator', but in the sense of 'one who binds or ties something' (it would only first be applied to the reptile fifty years later, in the 1590s). In 1538 he produced the first-ever Latin–English dictionary. It was a timely moment to publish such a book: the English Reformation had seen the Latin mass removed from churches up and down the country to be replaced with English-language services, and 1538 was also the year in which Henry VIII authorized an official English translation of the Bible (the so-called 'Great Bible') which appeared on church lecterns the following year.

Elyot's own view on the Reformation, however, was far from gung-ho. As well as being close friends with the Catholic martyr Thomas More, Elyot appears to have shared that statesman's stance on the king's divorce from Catherine of Aragon and subsequent marriage to Anne Boleyn. In 1533, the year Henry and Anne married, Elyot described the Reformation as 'a great cloud which is likely to be a great storm when it falls'. How right he was: two years later, More would be executed for refusing to acknowledge Henry as head of the newly established Church of England.

What is perhaps most significant about Elyot's role in all this is not what he said so much as how he said it. He titled one of his pamphlets *Pasquil the Playne* and he was known and admired for his plain speaking – or, rather, plain writing. In 1531, he wrote *The Boke Named the Governour*. Dedicated to Henry VIII, it's an instruction manual for young men of the governing classes, telling them how they ought to behave. It's essentially a 'how-to' guide for the gentry, and much of Elyot's book was highly influenced by Erasmus. It's been called the first book written in recognizably modern English prose, as opposed to Middle English.

But this was a dangerous time to be speaking one's mind plainly. Elyot was perhaps lucky to have fallen from grace so quietly, as it meant he survived long enough not only to compile his dictionary but also to develop his no-nonsense writing style. Yet his obscurity on the political scene also unfortunately means that his name has not endured as More's has. These days, if readers encounter Elyot's writing at all it is likely to be without realizing: his descendant and namesake, the poet Thomas Stearns Eliot, quotes from *The Boke Named the Governour* in his 1940 poem 'East Coker', the second of his *Four Quartets*.

## ✧ A Renaissance Bestseller ✧

Elyot's guide on how to be the perfect Renaissance gentleman wasn't the first such book, and may well have owed something to a book published a year earlier: *On Civility in Children*, a work by the Dutch scholar Erasmus. (Erasmus' book itself owed something to *The Courtier*, a work by Italian author Baldassare Castiglione written earlier in the sixteenth century.) Like *The Boke Named the Governour*, it's a conduct guide for the sixteenth century, offering advice on how to behave in a way befitting a man of good standing (and it is squarely aimed at men, or boys). Erasmus, like his friend Thomas More, was something of an all-round scholar: witty, educated, inventive, and a humanist. Born in Rotterdam some time in the late 1460s, he became a respected biblical scholar (preparing new Greek and Latin versions of the New Testament), as well as an author on everything from literary style to superstitious folly (his celebrated *In Praise of Folly*, written while Erasmus was staying at More's house in England).

What sort of advice did it offer? For one, wiping your nose on your sleeve was frowned upon. Offering your food, half-eaten, to someone else at the dining table was also a no-no. (Useful to get that learned.) Vomiting was preferable to holding the sick in your throat. Rocking back and forth on your chair was to be discouraged. 'Whoever does that gives the impression of constantly breaking, or trying to break, wind.' Well, obviously.

But it was more than just a book about table manners. Well actually, it wasn't *much* more: that was largely what it was about. But what's revealing is just how popular it was. Within the first ten years it was translated into twenty-two languages. It went through thirty editions in Erasmus' own lifetime, and a further hundred over the next three centuries. It was the bestseller of sixteenth-century Europe. Its popularity demonstrates that there was a burgeoning class of parents who needed guidance on how to raise their children, and Erasmus was the one to tell them how to do it: the Dr Benjamin Spock of his age. They wanted to ensure that their children were conversant with the dos and don'ts of sixteenth-century Europe, in a world where a breach of etiquette could, for this class of person, have serious consequences for their career at court. And if nothing else, it highlighted the importance of handkerchiefs and being sick.

## ❖ The First Female Playwright ❖

Ask someone who the first English female dramatist was, and you're likely to be met with one of three responses. 'No idea' might be the commonest, depending on whom you ask. Ask someone in the know, and the most popular answer would probably be Aphra Behn, who made a name for herself as one of the most popular dramatists during the Restoration era in the 1670s and 1680s. The other answer that might be offered is Mary Sidney, whose *Antonius* was published in 1592. But even Sidney doesn't get the title of the first English female dramatist. That honour – with a couple of provisos – goes to a woman named Joanna Lumley.

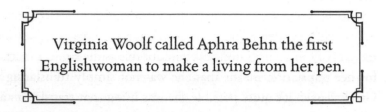

Virginia Woolf called Aphra Behn the first Englishwoman to make a living from her pen.

Joanna Lumley, also known as Lady Jane Lumley, was born in 1537 and died in 1578. Her translation of Euripides' *Iphigenia in Aulis*, which she probably made from the original Greek, was written (though never completed) in the 1550s when she was still a teenager, though it was first published only in 1909. *Iphigenia in Aulis* was the most translated Greek tragedy in the sixteenth century, and Erasmus – he of the conduct book about vomiting and breaking wind – had produced a popular Latin translation a few decades before.

But the date of composition and Lumley's choice of play are both suggestive. *Iphigenia in Aulis* is a play about a father sacrificing his daughter in order to win a war: Agamemnon orders the death of his own daughter, Iphigenia, in order to appease the goddess Artemis so that fair winds will enable him to sail off to the Trojan War. Around the time that Lumley is believed to have been at work on her translation of the Iphigenia story, another Lady Jane born in the same year as Lumley, Lady Jane Grey, was being installed on the throne by her politically ambitious father-in-law, the Duke of Northumberland. More than their given names and years of birth linked the women: they were first cousins. Famously, Jane Grey would rule

England for only nine days, and Bloody Mary, upon acceding to the throne, would have her imprisoned and, just to make sure, beheaded.

Northumberland sacrificed his own daughter-in-law for his own political ambition, and it's not hard to see a parallel with the tragedy of Iphigenia. Lumley's choice of this as the subject matter for her translation means that she was not simply translating a Greek classic; it's quite possible she was using that translation as a covert way of commenting on contemporary political events. Not only was *Iphigenia* the first known English translation of a Greek text, it was the first dramatic work in English that was written by a woman. It can also be read as a commentary on a contemporary real-life tragedy involving another woman named Lady Jane.

## ✦ Unlocking the Sonnet ✦

The accession of Bloody Mary to the throne in 1553, after Lady Jane Grey's ill-fated and brief reign, sent all sorts of devout Protestant reformers into exile. One of these was a woman named Anne Locke.

Locke was the daughter of Stephen Vaughan, who was in Henry VIII's service at the same time as Thomas Elyot. Unlike Elyot, Vaughan fully supported the Protestant Reformation – probably a bit too enthusiastically, given that the 1530s were a time when overzealous reformers could come to a sticky end as easily as ardent Catholics. His daughter Anne was born in around 1530 and inherited her father's reforming zeal. When she grew up she married Henry Locke, who shared the Vaughan family's passion for Protestant reform. In 1553 the Scottish reformer John Knox stayed with the Lockes, until the accession of Catholic Bloody Mary sent him into self-exile on the Continent. Anne and her husband joined Knox in Switzerland in 1557, taking their two young children with them. Their daughter died four days after they arrived in Geneva. The Lockes didn't stay long in Switzerland, and following the death of Mary I a year later, they returned to England. But Locke stayed in touch with Knox: Robert Louis Stevenson even argued that Anne Locke was the woman Knox loved more than any other.

Although she had not received a formal education – English schools were still all-male affairs – Locke had been taught the essentials, and could read and write well in several languages. This led to her translating some of the sermons of another Protestant Reformer, John Calvin, which were published in 1560.

But what's particularly interesting is the sequence of twenty-six sonnets that she included in the book of sermons. Titled *A Meditation of a Penitent Sinner: Written in Maner of A Paraphrase upon the 51. Psalme of David*, it's the first sonnet sequence written in English, published over twenty years before Sir Philip Sidney wrote his *Astrophil and Stella* and over thirty years before Shakespeare began his sonnets.

Locke's authorship of the sonnets only became widely accepted by scholars recently, and for a long time the general view was that Knox had written them. Locke helped to fan the flames of speculation, claiming in her preface to the sonnets that they were the work of a 'friend' and she was merely including them in her volume. (This is not the last time in this chapter that the prefatory material to a book of sonnets will cause wild speculation.) But the work appears to have been all Locke's, although, as the full title of the sequence suggests, the poems are a paraphrase of the sentiments expressed in the 51st Psalm.

The sonnets follow the rhyme scheme for the English sonnet developed by the Earl of Surrey in the 1540s, and more famously used by Shakespeare in his sonnets. Although the English form of the poem is commonly known as the Shakespearean sonnet, Shakespeare didn't invent it. Locke's poems, then, represent not merely the first cycle of sonnets written in English but also some of the first 'English sonnets', adopting the new rhyme scheme rather than copying the older Italian form.

## ✧ Beware the Cat ✧

Printers tend to get overlooked in the annals of literary history. Writers – if lucky – are praised for creating their work, and publishers are occasionally recognized (not to mention financially rewarded) for bringing that work to the world's attention, but the humble printer – almost the last link in the great chain of book-making – often languishes in obscurity. The sixteenth-century printer's assistant William Baldwin is more overlooked than most, and the fact that his name is not widely known is even more baffling given that he was a writer as well as a printer. He was the author of the first English sonnet ever to be printed, in around 1547. Others had written sonnets before Baldwin, such as the Earl of Surrey and Thomas Wyatt, but they had only been circulated in manuscript form and weren't published until the 1550s. Not only that, but Baldwin was the author of the very first English novel – or one of the leading candidates for that honour, at any rate.

*Beware the Cat* was written by Baldwin in around 1553 – around the time when Lady Jane Grey was enjoying her nine days on the throne – but not published until 1570. There was a good reason for the delay: if 1550s England is remembered for one thing, it is the burning of hundreds of Protestant martyrs during the reign of the Catholic Mary I. *Beware the Cat* offers a strong line in anti-Catholic mockery and when Mary came to the throne in 1553, Baldwin doubtless realized that printing it would not, to put it mildly, be the wisest of career moves. But after Mary's death five years later, and with the accession of the Protestant Elizabeth I, the book – with its playful but pointed ridiculing of Catholic superstitions and rituals – clearly became popular with readers and was reprinted in 1584.

*Beware the Cat* is huge fun: a short book containing interwoven stories, the kind of 'Chinese box' method of storytelling, it features werewolves and talking cats, magic potions and books of occult lore, and fuses the oral tradition of nursery rhymes with the high learning of Latin. At one point, fearing that Mouse-slayer, who has been placed in a walnut shell (don't ask), is the Devil (well, of course), a hapless Catholic priest slips on the poor cat and goes hurtling into a crowd of people, landing with his face in the 'bare arse' of a boy who has just 'beshit himself'. That's the sort of thing you won't find in *Middlemarch*.

*Beware the Cat* appears to be the origin of the term 'Grimalkin' for a witch's cat (later more famously used by Shakespeare in *Macbeth*).

Baldwin was also the editor and principal author of *The Mirror for Magistrates*, the book of 'lives' or tragedies that would go on to influence Shakespeare among other writers. But *Beware the Cat* is the one longer work by him that can be confidently identified as solely his work. It shares much with Thomas More's earlier *Utopia* – the structure, the style, the satiric tone – but with two important exceptions: its anti-Catholic content marks it out as a post-Reformation Protestant work, and crucially it's written not in Latin but English.

*Beware the Cat* is a remarkably rich, layered, playful and inventive book: not bad for England's first attempt at a novel. Indeed, one might go so far as to say that it's the first Gothic novel. Although that mantle usually goes to Horace Walpole's *The Castle of Otranto* (to which we'll come in due course), one of the odd things about Baldwin's novel is the way in which it anticipates, not so much the early Gothic novels of continental castles and crypts as conceived by Walpole and Ann Radcliffe, but the later Gothic strategies utilized to such effect in Victorian texts such as *Dracula* and *Strange Case of Dr Jekyll and Mr Hyde*. Like those classic works of late nineteenth-century fiction, *Beware the Cat* exposes the darker undercurrents found in London: it brings the Gothic home to England. It is also hugely tongue-in-cheek, containing marginal glosses where none are needed, as if the editor of the work (Baldwin himself) is treating the text as a scholarly work of arcane lore.

If Baldwin's name is remembered at all it tends to be for his role in editing *The Mirror for Magistrates*, but *Beware the Cat* is his masterpiece and represents his greatest contribution to English fiction. And it has cats. What more does one need?

## ❖ Shakespeare's Kyd ❖

In 1589, a young writer named Thomas Nashe, fresh from the University of Cambridge and newly arrived in London, had dreams of writing for the theatre. He appears to have wasted little time before setting about attacking those playwrights working on the London stage whom he deemed arrogant (given that he was barely twenty-one at the time, the enormous irony of his words seems to have been lost on Nashe himself). That same year, he published a blistering attack on upstart writers who 'think to out-brave better pens with the swelling bombast of a bragging blank verse'.

Although he didn't mention names, Nashe made it clear that his tirade was directed at a rival playwright of humble origins who had received only a grammar-school education, but nevertheless considered himself sufficiently educated to write plays that could rival those penned by university wits like Robert Greene, Christopher Marlowe and (in his own mind if no one else's) Nashe himself. Nashe went on: 'if you entreat him [i.e. this unnamed playwright] fair in a frosty morning, he will afford you whole *Hamlets*, I should say handfuls of tragical speeches'.

If Nashe's screed was motivated by envy, he was oddly – and prophetically – right to harbour such bad feeling: his own contribution to poetic drama would prove negligible, and perhaps the most interesting thing about his work, the above broadside excepted, is his use of the now-ubiquitous word 'email' (an obscure anglicization of the French term for enamel) in an otherwise unremarkable book of 1594, *The Terrors of the Night*.

But what is noteworthy about his attack on the humble playwright above is that Nashe is referring not to Shakespeare, but to someone else. Thomas Kyd was nine years older than Nashe and six years older than Shakespeare, and had already had at least one successful play performed on the London stage: *The Spanish Tragedy*, the earliest English example of the popular bloody revenge tragedy genre, had been first performed sometime in the 1580s, possibly in 1588. (Given the Spanish focus of Kyd's play, it is curious to note that this was also the year that Francis Drake defeated the Armada.) But Kyd was also most probably the author of a play called *Hamlet* that was first performed around the same time, and had certainly been performed by 1589, when Nashe launched his diatribe against the *Hamlet* author.

Sadly, this earlier play of *Hamlet* – commonly known as the *Ur-Hamlet*, from the German prefix '*Ur*' meaning 'prototype' or 'original' – has been lost and we know little about it. From contemporary references, however, we do know a handful of interesting facts: that there was a play about Hamlet performed in London over a decade before Shakespeare wrote his play *Hamlet*, that this early play focused on the theme of revenge, and that – like Shakespeare's later version – it featured a ghost. We know these last two things because in 1596 a writer named Thomas Lodge, in his book *Wit's Miserie and the World's Madness*, mentioned 'the ghost which cried so miserably at the theatre, like an oyster-wife, Hamlet, revenge!' This is five years before Shakespeare's *Hamlet* was first performed.

The fact that the earlier play was lost has not stopped critics from speculating about its influence on Shakespeare's play. T. S. Eliot used it as a stick to beat the Bard with, claiming that Shakespeare's *Hamlet* was an artistic failure because he struggled to rework Kyd's earlier, lost play into an emotionally convincing portrayal of the central character's odd relationship with his mother. William Empson went so far as to claim that the emotional excesses in Shakespeare's *Hamlet* were a deliberate parody of Kyd's original, the style of which had probably become outdated and laughable by 1601 when Shakespeare wrote his version.

> The first London theatre, the Red Lion, was built in 1567, when Shakespeare was three.

The 1580s were really the first great decade of English theatre. Throughout the Middle Ages, plays had been Catholic entertainments put on in town squares on holy feast days and other special occasions, dramatizing – usually in rather flat, functional dialogue – key events from the Bible such as the Crucifixion and Nativity. It was thanks to the Reformation that things changed. These old Popish displays were deemed unsuitable and offensive, and in their place arose the new phenomenon of the London playhouses. The Golden Age of English theatre, beginning in the 1580s, would see numerous playwrights take up their quills – Shakespeare, Christopher Marlowe, Ben Jonson, John Webster – but Kyd represents a decisive development in that he was one of the first known playwrights writing for the London stage whose work was clearly both popular and influential. Unfortunately, not popular enough to survive, at least in the case of the *Ur-Hamlet*.

Elizabethan plays were circulated in manuscript, but few people would possess a copy of an entire play, unless they were published. After all, copying out a whole manuscript many times over for each cast-member would be time-consuming when you had better things to do – such as lines to learn, and a show to rehearse and put on – so actors in plays would instead receive copies of only those scenes in which they had lines. These lines would be given to the actors on rolls of paper, which is why we now refer to an actor's part as a 'role' (from the French for such a roll of paper).

Sometimes early published versions of Elizabethan plays would be pieced together by several actors who would endeavour to remember – or, as was often the case, misremember – the lines from the play. This is probably why the 'bad' quarto of Shakespeare's *Hamlet*, published in 1603 a couple of years after the play was first staged, renders the celebrated line from Hamlet's famous soliloquy not as 'To be, or not to be: that is the question' but as 'To be or not to be, I there's the point.' Thank goodness others had a better memory, or better manuscripts.

Sadly, having helped to inspire perhaps the greatest work of English drama, Kyd didn't live long enough to see what Shakespeare did with his *Hamlet*. A known associate of the troublemaker Christopher Marlowe, Kyd was arrested and taken to the Tower of London, where he was interrogated about his fellow playwright under torture. He never recovered, and died a short while afterwards, in 1594.

## ✧ Who Is Mr W. H.? ✧

The dedication to the 1609 edition of *Shakespeare's Sonnets* must be the most baffling and elusive piece of prefatory material to a book that has ever been printed. You'd be hard-pushed to find another single page of text that has generated so much commentary yet without yielding a convincing solution. Critics and biographers remain divided. Who is the mysterious 'Mr. W. H.' to whom the volume is dedicated?

The dedication reads:

TO.THE.ONLIE.BEGETTER.OF.
THESE.INSVING.SONNETS.
MR.W.H.ALL.HAPPINESSE.
AND.THAT.ETERNITIE.
PROMISED.
BY.
OVR.EVER-LIVING.POET.
WISHETH.
THE.WELL-WISHING.
ADVENTVRER.IN.
SETTING.FORTH.
T.T.

The other initials, 'T. T.', are easier to decipher: they almost certainly refer to Thomas Thorpe, the publisher of the sonnets. Thorpe is thanking the dedicatee for being the 'onlie begetter' of the sonnets. But what does 'begetter' mean here, and does that help us to solve the mystery of who 'Mr. W. H.' was?

Numerous candidates have been proposed. Many scholars have assumed that the word 'begetter' means 'inspirer', and that the dedication refers to the 'Fair Youth' to whom many of the sonnets are addressed (it isn't as widely known as it should be that 'Shall I compare thee to a summer's day?', perhaps the most famous romantic line in all of English literature, is addressed by the male poet to a young man). William Herbert, the Earl of Pembroke, is a leading candidate for the 'Fair Youth', given that his initials fit, and he was later the dedicatee of the First Folio which gathered together Shakespeare's works into one volume in 1623. The problem with Pembroke is that dedications to members of the nobility were usually rather obsequious at the time (they still are, when they appear in books at all), so would a mere publisher dare address an earl as 'Mr'? The same goes for another candidate proposed for 'Mr. W. H.', Henry Wriothesley, the Earl of Southampton, who had already had two of Shakespeare's narrative poems dedicated to him. The argument goes that his initials were reversed (whether by accident or design) – 'H. W.' became 'W. H.' But again, the argument falls down when we consider that Wriothesley (pronounced 'rizzly') was an earl, not a plain old 'mister' or 'master'.

Oscar Wilde put forward his own theory – or rather, his take on an earlier theory first proposed in the eighteenth century – in an 1889 story, 'The Portrait of Mr. W. H.'. In Wilde's story, a number of characters become convinced that the initials refer to Willie Hughes, a boy actor in Shakespeare's theatre company. The sonnets therefore reveal a passionate homoerotic love affair between Shakespeare and the enigmatic Hughes. Puns on 'will' and 'hews' (i.e. 'hues', meaning shades or colours) in the sonnets provide some internal, if conjectural, evidence for the theory. The main problem is that there's no evidence Willie Hughes ever existed, which is a somewhat unfortunate drawback.

Other theories have been proposed by would-be literary detectives. In his 1964 book *Mr W. H.*, the self-styled literary sleuth Leslie Hotson claimed to have identified the *Sonnets'* dedicatee in William Hatcliffe, a Lincolnshire man. Others have argued that 'W. H.' stands for 'Who He', and was thus merely a publisher's ploy to encourage public speculation concerning the identity of the mystery figure.

All such theories seem to run with the idea that this dedication – perhaps the most famous in all of English literature – is addressed to the man who inspired Shakespeare to write the sonnets. But is that really the case? Numerous commentators, including Bertrand Russell, thought otherwise. During Shakespeare's time, 'begetter' was more likely to mean 'writer' than 'inspirer'. Poets 'begat' their poems, like a father siring a child. Could Shakespeare himself be the person to whom the dedication is addressed? Thorpe may have published Shakespeare's sonnets without the poet's permission, so this dedication could have been Thorpe's way of keeping the Bard sweet. So, for 'W. H.' read 'W. S.'

But if this is the case, why doesn't the dedication address itself to 'Mr. W. S.'? William Shakespeare, no nobleman, would certainly have been addressed as 'Mr.', but 'W. H.' makes no sense. The idea of a misprint, however – or a printer's misreading of a handwritten 'S' as 'H' – is not as far-fetched as it might seem. In *The Genius of Shakespeare*, Jonathan Bate cites the example of a Thomas Goffe play from the period called *The Raging Turke*, which was actually printed with 'THE RANING TURKE' in big letters on its title page. If that slipped through, why not 'W. H.'?

So, for all that, what is perhaps the most enigmatic dedication in all of English literature may be nothing more than a publisher addressing the author of the poems that follow and trying to avoid legal trouble resulting from printing a poet's work without his blessing. But the truth is that we will never quite know for sure; and the mystery surrounding Shakespeare's sonnets is likely to continue to exercise its power over readers for years to come.

# ✧ Quixotic ✧

On the day that Shakespeare departed the world in Stratford-upon-Avon, 23 April 1616, another literary great was being laid to rest in Spain: Miguel de Cervantes. The date of his death is commonly given as 23 April, but in fact he had died the day before. A year earlier, he had completed the second part of his masterpiece *Don Quixote*. It was hugely popular across Europe and part of it even served as the source material for one of Shakespeare's late collaborations, the lost play *Cardenio*.

Several words now in common use, namely 'quixotic' and 'lothario', have their roots in the novel. It was a pioneering work of fiction, an early example of the novel, and even postmodern long before the term had been invented. The *Monty Python* crew may have been fans: it's been argued that their famous Cheese Shop sketch owes something to *Don Quixote*.

Alonso Quixano, the 'Don Quixote' of the book's title, is a hidalgo (member of the minor Spanish nobility) approaching fifty years of age and living in La Mancha with his niece and housekeeper. He's filled his head with the tales of chivalry he's read, and unfortunately believes that all of these romances are true. Inspired by the tales of knightly heroism he's been devouring, Quixano decides to become a knight himself, and off he goes, tilting at windmills (that is, cowering from them, because he believes they're monsters).

*Don Quixote* is actually not one book, but two: the original adventure and its sequel, written a decade after the original book. In the interim between the appearance of the first volume in 1605 and the second in 1615, a rip-off spin-off merchant named Alonso Fernández de Avellaneda had stolen

Cervantes' characters (no copyright laws then) and written an inferior sequel to the first book, 'The Second Volume of the Ingenious Knight Don Quixote de la Mancha', which was published in 1614. If there was going to be a proper follow-up book, Cervantes decided, he was the one to write it, and so set to work on part two of his book.

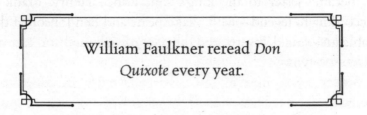

William Faulkner reread *Don Quixote* every year.

The narrator of *Don Quixote* credits the story to a Muslim historian named Cide Hamete Benengeli (which means 'aubergine' in Arabic). Benengeli never existed – it was a literary conceit on Cervantes' part.

Cervantes had lost his left hand in the naval battle of Lepanto in 1571. He and his brother were captured by pirates in 1575 – and sold as slaves to the King of Algiers. They would remain slaves for five years, until the ransom was eventually paid. Cervantes also helped to prepare the Spanish Armada for its attack on England in 1588.

*Don Quixote* is also the gross-out comedy of seventeenth-century Spain. The title character shits himself in a cage at one point. At another moment, he inadvertently exposes himself to young ladies who stumble into his bedroom. Both Sancho Panza and Don Quixote throw up in each other's face. It's irreverent, bawdy, vulgar – and exceedingly modern. And there's a lot more than windmills in it.

# ✧ A Collection of Crudities ✧

The world of books is home to many unsung heroes and forgotten names. Yet even if we grant this, it seems odd that the name of Thomas Coryat should be so unknown. In his day, he was big news. He went to the court of King James I, became jester to the king's son, Prince Henry, drank – according to legend – with Shakespeare and Ben Jonson at the fabled Mermaid Tavern, and did a lot of walking. And I mean a *lot* of walking.

In 1608 he walked all the way from London to Venice and back, in the same pair of shoes. When he arrived home he hung the shoes in the local church; Shakespeare may have been referring to them when, in *Measure for Measure*, the Clown Pompey mentions 'brave Master Shoe-tie the great traveller'. Coryat gave himself the sobriquet 'the Odcombian Leg-stretcher', after the Somerset village where he grew up. Nobody in Jacobean England knew how to stretch their legs quite like Coryat.

He documented his Italian travels in a wonderfully eccentric book, *Coryat's Crudities: Hastily gobled up in Five Moneth's Travels*, which appeared in 1611, the same year as the King James Bible. The beginning of the book featured an imposingly large number of dedications, both in prose and verse, with contributions from Coryat's friends and associates including Ben Jonson, Michael Drayton, John Donne and Inigo Jones. (These commendatory verses are arranged in a number of unusual styles, to match the eccentricity of the book's author: there's even a poem in the shape of an egg.) What's remarkable about these poems in praise of Coryat is how many of them *don't* praise him, but instead poke fun at him and his eccentricities. Coryat sportingly includes these verses too. He seems to have known everyone: anyone who was anyone in early seventeenth-century England queued up to sing his praises – or, as is often the case, to do the opposite. The book has a *lot* of dedicatory verses. You have to wade through nearly half of the first volume before you get to the start of Coryat's book.

Once the book proper begins, it yields a host of surprising things. Coryat recorded that he had seen the Italians eating their food with a small fork. When members of King James's court read of this custom, they duly adopted it. This is how the idea was introduced to England of eating meals with a knife and fork. (Coryat's friends duly nicknamed him *Furciferus*, 'fork-bearer'.) Coryat also noted the Italian custom of shielding oneself from the sun's glare by using a strange contraption whose name meant, literally, 'little shadow'. It's the first appearance in England of the word *umbrella* and would signal the beginning of a new English habit: using such a device to keep the rain off when outdoors. The same book also introduced the William Tell myth to English readers.

> Umbrellas would only become widely used as protection against the rain in the eighteenth century: the first Londoner to carry one, Jonas Hanway, was mocked for doing so.

Coryat was probably the first Briton to undertake what became known as a 'Grand Tour' of Europe. But eventually all the travelling caught up with him. In December 1617

Coryat died in India, his death supposedly brought on by too much beer and meat in the hot climate. In effect, he became the first Englishman to die of 'Delhi belly'. He was also arguably the first travel writer in the English language. We should remember his name next time we're handling a fork at mealtime or reaching for our umbrellas on a rainy day.

# THE AGE OF ENLIGHTENMENT

On 1 January 1660, a 27-year-old naval administrator named Samuel Pepys wrote the first entry in what would become his world-famous diary. Partly what makes the diary so entertaining is Pepys's personality: his confession of his own weaknesses, his refreshing frankness. But the diary is also the chronicle of a busy decade in English history. It's well known that Pepys documents the Great Plague, the Great Fire of London and the Dutch raid on the Medway, but it's often the little day-to-day details that make the diary so interesting. Pepys's diary contains one of the first references to a Punch and Judy show in England, as well as a description of a watch fitted with an alarm – a cutting-edge innovation for the time.

Pepys was also an avid book-collector. Among his possessions at his death was another famous person's diary – the almanac that had belonged to Sir Francis Drake, hero of the Spanish Armada. (Pepys reportedly liked to arrange his books not by their subject but by their size, which must have made his shelves look nice but rendered it rather difficult to locate the book he was after.) By Pepys's time, printed books had become more widely available and could be produced more cheaply. A gentleman with the right income could amass a considerable library.

After the Renaissance, the Enlightenment was the next major cultural and scientific leap forward for the Western world. It really got going with the scientific revolution of the seventeenth century, which included, among other discoveries, Galileo's proof that the planets of our solar system orbited the sun (rather than the planets and the sun being in Earth's orbit), Newton's work on the gravitational force, and the discovery of calculus (this was Newton again, but also Gottfried Leibniz: the two men squabbled over who had got there first). Much philosophical reflection followed, with figures including David Hume and Immanuel Kant puzzling over big ideas such as the rational mind, our relationship with the physical world, and the nature of free will.

But it was also a time when littler, but nevertheless important, discoveries and developments occurred. In September 1660, Pepys recorded in his diary that he had drunk his very first cup of tea, signalling the arrival of a new drink from faraway China that the English would take to their hearts – and their mouths – with great gusto. A new upstart literary form, the novel, sought to reflect the world's new scientific confidence in empiricism (examining the physical world oneself, rather than relying on cold logic alone, or someone else's word for it), as well as Europe's interest in sailing the world and discovering more about it (and, it must be added, colonizing or enslaving much of it in the process). The novel became the perfect form for telling the story of how an individual makes their way in the world: Robinson Crusoe, Moll Flanders, Tom Jones. People also sought to catalogue things: in France there was Diderot's *Encyclopédie*, in Scotland the *Encyclopedia Britannica*, and in England Samuel Johnson's *Dictionary* (of which more later), all compiled within a few decades of each other.

This chapter takes in some of the key developments that occurred in Britain and Ireland between the mid-seventeenth and mid-eighteenth centuries, during the age of Enlightenment and reason. Two words loom large: exploration and classification. So if you have your telescope and microscope at the ready, we'll voyage off into the unknown – or at least, the little-known.

## ✧ The Original Debunker ✧

It has become second nature to us to debunk myths and question and examine widely held beliefs. But such a pursuit is nothing new. A seventeenth-century man was doing it, and an eager public was reading about it, over 350 years ago. The man in question was Sir Thomas Browne (1605–82), who, fittingly, provides us with the first recorded use of the word 'misconception'.

Browne first came to my attention as a prolific coiner of words, and although we cannot be sure he was the very first person to derive or invent all of the following, the *Oxford English Dictionary* credits him with the first recorded use of numerous words now in regular or everyday use, including (and these are only the most familiar ones): 'ambidextrous', 'antediluvian', 'approximate', 'biped', 'bisect', 'botanical', 'capillary', 'carnivorous', 'coma', 'compensate', 'complicated', 'cynicism', 'discrimination', 'electricity', 'elevator', 'executive', 'ferocious', 'gypsum', 'hallucination', 'inactivity', 'insecurity', 'medical', 'nonexistence', 'perspire', 'prairie', 'praying mantis', 'precocious', 'prefix', 'presumably', 'secretion', 'selection', 'subsidence', 'temperamental', 'transferable', 'transgressive' and 'ulterior'. He also provides one of the earliest uses of 'computer' (the word originally referred to a person who made calculations), though not, as has sometimes been claimed, the very first.

Browne was born in Cheapside in London in 1605. During the English Civil War he worked as a doctor in Norwich – a Parliamentary city, although Browne himself remained a Royalist. He wrote on a range of topics, including religion (his *Religio Medici*, or 'the religion of a doctor', proved hugely successful when it appeared in the 1640s), urn-burial (on which he wrote a famous treatise) and various topics pertaining to the natural world.

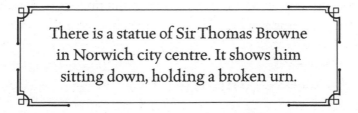

There is a statue of Sir Thomas Browne in Norwich city centre. It shows him sitting down, holding a broken urn.

It was this last subject that he took as the theme of his most ambitious work, *Pseudodoxia Epidemica*, which was published in 1646, although it was so popular it went through many more editions during Browne's lifetime. The full title of this book is *Pseudodoxia Epidemica or Enquiries into very many received tenets and commonly presumed truths*, although it is sometimes known simply as *Vulgar Errors*. Its purpose was to examine the widely held superstitions and beliefs of the time, and to correct those that were false.

In order to do this, and in the empirical spirit popularized by Sir Francis Bacon earlier in the century, Browne conducted his own experiments wherever possible. In order to determine whether, as contemporary wisdom had it, spiders and toads repelled each other, he placed several spiders into a glass container with a toad. The result? The spiders walked over the toad's body; the toad, in turn, ate the spiders. Among the other errors of the day which he refuted were the belief that elephants had four knees, that crystal was merely very hard ice (yes, some people really believed that), and that if you rub a magnet with garlic you remove some of its magnetic power. Browne challenges and corrects these beliefs with wit and humour, writing in ornate but accessible prose. He was a one-man debunking machine. When diarist John Evelyn visited Browne's house, he described it as a 'cabinet of curiosities'. 'Curiosity' was Browne's game.

## ✧ Another Diary ✧

Some people are just born at the right time. If you were a diarist, the seventeenth century was a particularly good time to be alive, though also a potentially dangerous one. The 1640s brought the English Civil War, and in the 1660s, following the Restoration of the monarchy and the accession of Charles II, there was the Great Plague, the Great Fire of London and the invasion of the Dutch fleet, all occurring within a year or two of each other.

One such diarist lived through these interesting times and documented many of the key events of the age – though the diary in which his observations appeared would not be published for over a century, in 1818. I'm talking about John Evelyn (1620–1706), whose daily jottings would soon be overshadowed by the publication of a more famous diary written by naval administrator and cheese-burier Samuel Pepys, in 1825. (That's not a euphemism: during the Great Fire, Pepys buried his expensive Parmesan cheese in his garden to save it from the flames.)

But the publication of Evelyn's diary was partly the reason the world took any notice of Pepys's in the first place. It ignited the public interest in the intellectual life of the seventeenth century, as well as its historical events: the Fire, the Plague, the Civil War. It's a vivid account of the second half of the seventeenth century. Pepys only kept his diary for a decade, from 1660 until 1669, but Evelyn's spanned much of his adult life. Highlights include the funeral of Oliver Cromwell in 1658, at which, Evelyn records, nobody cried except the dogs (a Royalist rather than Parliamentarian, Evelyn may have been a slightly biased reporter here).

From 1660, after over a decade without a monarch, England would once again have a king in the shape of Charles II. The decades that followed would become known as the Restoration, from the restoring of the monarchy, and Charles would be dubbed 'the Merry Monarch'. Along with Pepys's diary, Evelyn's journal is a valuable document from this period.

Evelyn's diary is also an important record of England's – and Europe's – growing interest in all things scientific. Like Pepys, Evelyn left behind a substantial library when he died, and his interests – like Thomas Browne's before him – were wide-ranging. It is in Evelyn that we find the first reference in English to the new feature called a 'green-house', for growing one's own vegetables and plants. (His diary also contains the earliest reference to a wheelchair.) Evelyn also wrote what is probably the first book about the problem of air pollution in London, *Fumifugium*, published in 1661. Given the fact that Evelyn had a lifelong interest in gardening and growing vegetables, it's pleasing to note that his 1699 book *Acetaria* is the first book ever written about salad.

When the Royal Society was granted a Royal Charter to publish books in 1662, the first volume it printed was a book by John Evelyn. It was called *Sylva*, and bore the subtitle *A Discourse of Forest-Trees and the Propagation of Timber*. The second book the Society published was called *Micrographia* and was by a young man named Robert Hooke.

## ✧ Drunk Fleas and Microscopes ✧

History has not been kind to Robert Hooke, because Isaac Newton wasn't kind to him. Hooke endured a vicious rivalry with Newton – at least, it was vicious on Newton's part – and cunning Isaac set about expunging Hooke from the historical record. He even had all the portraits of his rival destroyed. As a result, we have no definite idea of what Hooke even looked like. Ironically, it was in a letter to Hooke that Newton penned his famous line (borrowed from the medieval philosopher Bernard of Chartres), 'If I have seen further, it is by standing on the shoulders of giants.' Ironic, because Hooke was one of the giants on whose shoulders Newton had, at least in part, stood.

Hooke started out as assistant to Robert Boyle, author of *The Sceptical Chymist* (1661) and originator of Boyle's Law. Indeed, Hooke's work with Boyle – particularly their experiments with air-pumps – helped to lay the groundwork for Boyle's discovery of the natural law that bears his name. Hooke would go on to do many things, including helping to rebuild London after the Great Fire of 1666. He speculated that there might be evidence in the earth's strata for earlier life forms, over a century before the vogue for prehistoric fossil-hunting; he even proposed that species might alter over time. This was nearly two centuries before Darwin would publish his theory of evolution by natural selection. And Hooke helped to inspire Newton's work on the inverse square law of planetary attraction. Indeed, along with a dispute over optics, this is what led to them falling out, when Hooke claimed Newton had not credited him with the idea.

But Hooke's most important work was undertaken with science's new toy: the microscope. By modern standards the device that Hooke constructed is a primitive thing, but at the time it was a revelation. His book *Micrographia* showed readers for the first time – through the use of graphic illustrations – what living things looked like, close up. He shoved anything and everything under his lens, and recorded what he observed: plants, insects, cheese, even his own urine. Sometimes his methods were unusual but inspired. The famous giant illustration of a flea included in Hooke's book was made possible by brandy, which is what Hooke used to get his blood-sucking model to stay still under his microscope: as Hooke records, 'I gave it a Gill of Brandy, or Spirit of Wine, which after a while e'en knock'd him down dead drunk.'

It was in *Micrographia* that Hooke coined the word 'cell' for the biological unit. Observing them under his microscope, Hooke thought they looked similar to the cells of a honeycomb, and a new sense of the word was born. *Micrographia* was probably the first science book to become a bestseller since Euclid's

*Elements*, which had sold steadily since the printed book had come into being two centuries before. Samuel Pepys stayed up late reading it, pronouncing it to be 'the most ingenious book that I ever read in my life'. That is, probably, until he read Newton's groundbreaking *Principia* two decades later – a book which Pepys, in his capacity as President of the Royal Society, licensed for publication. In this as in so much else, Hooke was destined to be eclipsed and outstripped by prickly Newton.

> A number of useful words, among them 'diverge', 'door-mat', 'loosening', 'menagerie' and 'penumbra', made their debut in print in the *Micrographia*.

## ❖ A Trailblazer ❖

Few women writers have been more versatile than Margaret Cavendish. At a time when barely any women published work under their own name, Cavendish proudly slapped her signature on the title pages of the books she published, proclaiming her authorship but also her womanhood. And she wrote a great deal: volumes of poetry, closet dramas, autobiographical memoir, moral fables, and even prose discourses on science. Indeed, Cavendish was the first woman to attend a meeting of the Royal Society, another sign that her interests ranged beyond the literary into the (then almost exclusively male) realm of science. A Royalist, she spent a number of years living in exile in France following the English Civil War, during which time she had dinner with the eminent French philosopher Descartes. She might be described as a 'Renaissance woman', although historically speaking she belonged to the slightly later Restoration period, having been born in 1623 and writing much of her mature work in the second half of the seventeenth century.

Of all her many works, it is a short work of fiction called *The Blazing World* which is perhaps the most remarkable. It might be described as an early novella. Published in 1666, the year that London was literally ablaze with the Great Fire, Cavendish's book is a fictional account of a young woman who undertakes a fantastic voyage to another world, accessed via the North Pole. While she is sojourning in this fantasy world, Cavendish's female protagonist gets married to the Emperor, and converses with the various animal–human hybrids that inhabit the land: bird-men, bear-men, fish-men, worm-men. Recent scientific discoveries and developments are discussed, including the new invention of the microscope (Cavendish had almost certainly read Hooke's *Micrographia*, published the year before). In this alternate world, microscopy is inverted: the bear-men create a device which reduces large animals to a tiny fraction of their actual size, so that a whale appears the size of a sprat and a mighty elephant the size of a flea (another suggestive nod to Hooke's book).

Indeed, in these and other ways, *The Blazing World* oddly anticipates the looking-glass world of Lewis Carroll's *Alice* books, published two centuries later, and not just because both works involve a female protagonist leaving behind our own world for a fictional land in which our world is curiously inverted. Both works also appear to offer a commentary on contemporary scientific debates. Cavendish's inverted microscopes are a good example.

*The Blazing World* is in the utopian tradition, that genre named by Sir Thomas More a century and a half earlier. Indeed, it's the only work of utopian fiction written by a woman to be published in the whole of the seventeenth century. But it's also been called an early work of science fiction. Its legacy can perhaps most clearly be seen in Alan Moore's graphic novel sequence *The League of Extraordinary Gentlemen*, whose setting is a homage to Cavendish's blazing world.

Yet for many centuries, Cavendish's work was forgotten – left to moulder in the gloom of public libraries, in Virginia Woolf's memorable phrase. In *A Room of One's Own*, Woolf likens Cavendish to a cucumber that has spread itself over the roses and carnations in the garden, choking the poor flowers to death. Indeed, many commentators have approached Cavendish's work cautiously, as if half-afraid her books might suddenly turn around and bite their hand off. There is something subversive and daring about *The Blazing World*, particularly the way it transcends traditional genre boundaries. What is it? It is utopia, proto-science fiction, adventure story, scientific treatise and prose romance, all in one. And that is what lends it its monstrous appeal.

# ❖ A Fiennes Way to Travel ❖

Unlike Margaret Cavendish, Celia Fiennes – the author of a remarkable travel journal – was the daughter of a Parliamentarian who had supported Oliver Cromwell during the English Civil War. Fiennes was born in 1662, over a decade after the end of the Civil War and two years after the English monarchy had been restored and Charles II crowned king. (England had tried being kingless for eleven years between Parliament's execution of Charles I in 1649 and the return from exile of his son, Charles II, in 1660.)

In other respects, too, Fiennes was the mirror opposite of Margaret Cavendish. She never married. She showed no particular inclination for writing fiction or drama. But both women shared a passion for writing for the amusement of their families. During her twenties, Fiennes began travelling around England on horseback, with only a couple of her servants for company. She wrote about the places she visited, and regaled her relatives with her accounts of everything from Stonehenge in Wiltshire to Newcastle at the other end of the country. The travel journal was coming into fashion at the time, and Fiennes rode its wave magnificently, though she only documented her experiences for the benefit of her friends and relations and never sought to publish them.

Her journal is more than just a record of the landmarks and buildings she visited. For one thing, it reveals the danger and discomfort that awaited even the well-heeled traveller during the late seventeenth century. She tells us of how she put up with 'froggs and slow-worms and snailes' in the room in which she lodged at Ely, and of how she was held up by highwaymen near

Chester. But other things made her travels easier. In 1697, the year before she embarked on a 'Great Journey to Newcastle and to Cornwall', an act of parliament ordered signposts to be displayed at key crossroads to reduce the chances of travellers getting lost. (It wasn't a complete success: Fiennes still frequently ended up with no idea where she was.) A few centuries before this, in Margery Kempe's time, you generally needed special permission to wander the country, otherwise you ran the risk of being arrested as a vagrant. By the time Fiennes was riding around Britain, such meandering was positively encouraged. In the end she visited every single county in England, as well as Scotland and Wales – though she didn't much like either of them.

Fiennes was an early adopter of the spa treatment, visiting Harrogate to take the waters there. (She preferred the water at Bath, describing the smell at Harrogate as possessing an 'offencivness like carrion or a jakes' – that is, a toilet.) She visited numerous stately homes, a curiously modern pastime. Indeed, very little about Fiennes was *not* modern. She preferred the newer city of Nottingham to the centuries of history contained in a city like York. Unlike the Romantics who lived a century later, she had no real love of ruins, preferring instead the newer country houses and the bustling commercial centres of industry and trade. Mines, in particular, loom large in her journal.

Fiennes was writing over twenty years before Defoe published his more famous *Tour thro' the Whole Island of Great Britain* (1724–7), another early work of English travel writing. She was a pioneering figure in this regard. It's even been suggested that the nursery rhyme 'Ride a cock horse to Banbury Cross' was written about her: she is the 'fine lady [*Fiennes* lady?] upon a white horse', at least so the theory goes. It's a nice idea but unlikely.

It was a leading figure of the later Romantic movement, Robert Southey, who would first publish excerpts from her journal in 1812. The journal was only fully published as a book nearly eighty years later, when it appeared in an imperfect transcription as *Through England on a Side Saddle* in 1888. (A fuller, corrected edition eventually followed in 1947.) An appetite for adventure runs in the Fiennes blood: one of her descendants is the explorer Ranulph Fiennes.

## ✧ *Crusoe*: The Sequel ✧

Daniel Defoe's 1719 book *Robinson Crusoe*, often called the first English novel, is the tale of one man's survival on an apparently deserted island following a shipwreck. The longer, considerably less snappy title that appeared on the title page of the first edition in 1719 read: *The Life and Strange Surprizing Adventures of Robinson Crusoe, Of York, Mariner: Who lived Eight and Twenty Years, all alone in an un-inhabited Island on the Coast of America, near the Mouth of the Great River of Oroonoque; Having been cast on Shore by Shipwreck, wherein all the Men perished but himself. With An Account how he was at last as strangely deliver'd by Pyrates.*

The book didn't carry Defoe's name, and it was offered to the public as a true account of genuine events, documented by a real man named Crusoe. But readers were immediately sceptical. In the same year as the novel appeared, a man named Charles Gildon actually published *Robinson Crusoe Examin'd and Criticis'd*, in which he showed that Crusoe was made up and the events of the novel were fiction. (Few people were bothered by this, as the line between fiction and non-fiction had not yet become so important.)

> 'Crusoe' may have been taken from Timothy Cruso, who had been a classmate of Defoe's and who had gone on to write guidebooks.

The story of *Robinson Crusoe* is famous, but few people know about, let alone read, the *two* sequels to the book which Defoe wrote. *The Farther Adventures of Robinson Crusoe* followed later in the same year, with *Serious Reflections of Robinson Crusoe* published a year later in 1720. *Serious Reflections* is largely a repackaged collection of Defoe's non-fiction works published under the lucrative Crusoe brand, but *The Farther Adventures* deserves to be better known. This sequel sees Crusoe return to his island after the death of his wife in England; then, following the death of Man Friday, his faithful servant from the original book, he travels to Madagascar, the Far East and Siberia, before returning to England ten years later.

The real-life story of Alexander Selkirk was not Defoe's only source for *Robinson Crusoe*. Numerous scholars and historians, including Tim Severin in his book *Seeking Robinson Crusoe*, have challenged this widely held belief. Severin cites the case of a man named Henry Pitman, who wrote a short book recounting his adventures in the Caribbean following his escape from a penal colony and his subsequent shipwrecking and survival on a desert island. Pitman appears to have lived in the same area as Defoe, and Defoe may have met him in person and learned of his experiences first-hand. It is also revealing that both men had taken part in the Monmouth Rebellion of 1685. (Indeed, Defoe had only narrowly escaped being sentenced to death by the fearsome Judge Jeffreys.)

There is a real place called Robinson Crusoe Island, but it is not Robinson Crusoe's island. Let me explain: Defoe's island is located in the Caribbean, but the real place named Robinson Crusoe Island is in the south Pacific. It was so named because Selkirk *was* stranded in the Pacific. But fiction is so often more resonant than fact, and so the island is named after Defoe's character rather than the real man who actually lived there. Curiously, there *is* an Alexander Selkirk Island, located some 100 miles west of Robinson Crusoe Island, but it is little more than a rock.

## ✧ Swift Success ✧

A year after Defoe's sequel to *Robinson Crusoe* appeared, Jonathan Swift began working in earnest on his own travel adventure narrative involving a shipwreck, a lone traveller and an island (in fact, several islands). It was to be a satirical fantasy novel that would poke fun at the 'travellers' tales' which were popular at the time. The resulting book, published in 1726, bore the title *Travels into Several Remote Nations of the World. In Four Parts. By Lemuel Gulliver, First a Surgeon, and then a Captain of Several Ships*. We now know it, of course, as *Gulliver's Travels*. The book was a bestseller by any standards: 10,000 copies were sold in the first three weeks. It evidently struck a chord with readers right from the off.

Like *Robinson Crusoe, Gulliver's Travels* presented itself to the reader as a genuine account, recounting four voyages made by Lemuel Gulliver. The first (and most famous) of the four is to Lilliput, a land inhabited by tiny people. Gulliver is expelled from Lilliput by its diminutive inhabitants because he urinates on a fire to help put it out. Following this cock-up, his second voyage is to Brobdingnag, land of the giants – here the shoe's on the other foot and Gulliver is the little person. The third land, Laputa, a flying island in the tradition of More's *Utopia*, is a land whose inhabitants worship science above all else (Swift was highly suspicious of the modern world's faith in scientific advancement). The fourth of the lands Gulliver visits is the land of the Houyhnhnms, horses endowed with reason and the power of speech. Humans, by contrast, are filthy muck-flinging beasts known as 'Yahoos', later to give their name to an internet search engine. (George Orwell later pointed out that Swift liked horses because, of all the animals, the smell of their dung is the least offensive to humans. Curiously, Swift has been credited with authoring a pamphlet titled 'Human Ordure', which is signed on its title page 'Dr S—t', i.e. 'Shit' but also 'Swift'.)

When he arrives home, Gulliver realizes how much mankind resembles the Yahoos – and he swiftly (no pun intended) sinks into dejection, preferring to speak with the horses in his stable (which, unlike the Houyhnhnms, can't talk back).

Despite Swift's mockery and distrust of science, his novel was, sometimes inadvertently, at the forefront of scientific discovery. At one point he writes that the planet Mars is orbited by two moons. This seemed fanciful at the time, but the two moons were discovered 150 years later. (In honour of this piece of prophecy, a crater on one of the moons, Deimos, was named after Swift.) Pat

Rogers, in his essay 'Gulliver's Glasses', claims that Gulliver is the first protagonist in English fiction to wear spectacles – which he uses as shields when he visits the island of Blefuscu, another land inhabited by little people, and the inhabitants begin shooting arrows at him. Science isn't all bad, it would seem.

There have been numerous bowdlerized and sanitized versions of Swift's classic since it first appeared in 1726 – versions for children, with some of the more politically complex, or filthier, parts removed – but in fact the very first such cleaned-up edition of the novel was the first edition of 1726. To his horror, when Swift looked through the first edition it was to find that his publisher, Benjamin Motte, had deliberately toned down numerous sections of the narrative, especially those which were most pointedly satirizing contemporary events and which might land Swift – and, more to the point, Motte himself – in trouble. (It was also riddled with misprints.) It would be the 1730s before the book appeared as Swift intended.

We often celebrate great works of literature for their generosity of spirit: we talk of Shakespeare's 'humanity', of Wordsworth's empathy, George Eliot's humanistic ability to feel for another person. But Swift is in quite a different tradition. He was disgusted by us all with our filthy bodies and rotten, wrong-headed attitudes. Yet he wrote a great work of literature in *Gulliver's Travels*. Perhaps the key aspect of the novel here is its satire: it means that we can never be sure when Swift is being serious and when he is pulling our leg, when he is inviting us to share Gulliver's views and when he wishes us to long to clout the silly fool round the head. That, too, is one of the signs of a timeless novel: its multifaceted quality. *Gulliver's Travels* has more facets than you can shake a mucky stick at.

# ✧ The Disappearing Play ✧

British theatre in the 1730s was, it was widely felt, getting out of hand. A raft of young playwrights, led by Henry Fielding, were lampooning the country's leader – Sir Robert Walpole, the country's first de facto prime minister – and his government in a series of stage satires. Satire had been fine when it was confined to novels like *Gulliver's Travels* and, more importantly, wasn't putting Walpole's nose out of joint. Walpole was losing face (though he retained his majority in parliament) and decided that something had to be done, so he set about securing support for stage censorship.

Fortunately for him, he found just the ammunition he needed in a scurrilous new play called *The Golden Rump*, a copy of which Walpole allegedly acquired from a nervous stage manager. The play, a scatological satire of the British royal family, took aim at King George II, specifically his bowel problems: the set was reportedly planned to be a giant pair of buttocks, with characters making their entrance onto the stage through the anus. Walpole read excerpts aloud in the House of Commons, to drum up support for his moral crusade.

No copy of the play survives, but that's possibly because a copy never existed in the first place. Many commentators, including Fielding himself, accused Walpole of making the whole thing up. Real or not, *The Golden Rump* gave Walpole what he wanted, and from 1737 stage censorship was introduced in British theatres in the form of the Licensing Act. This act meant that the Lord Chamberlain had to read every play due to be performed on the British stage and make sure it did not contravene any laws regarding what was and wasn't allowed to be portrayed. Satire of the government and royalty was definitely out. Suddenly, British theatres were very boring places to be, at least in terms of new comedy. The Licensing Act explains why it's difficult to name many truly groundbreaking playwrights for the British stage (excepting a few names, such as Sheridan, Wilde, and Shaw) for the next 200 years.

The excesses of the 1730s led to curtailments of other kinds: it is well known that the United States introduced Prohibition in 1920, but London introduced a ban – albeit only on strong alcohol such as spirits – in response to the capital's gin problem in 1736. It would remain in force until 1743, when (much like the American prohibition on alcohol two centuries later) it was repealed, having been a resounding failure.

Oddly, though, the imposition of theatre censorship would be just about the best thing that could happen to English literature and the nation's print culture. Press freedoms were not similarly restricted, and the eighteenth century was truly the age of the newspaper: a new periodical seemed to spring up somewhere in the metropolis every day. *The Gentleman's Magazine*, the first English publication to style itself as a 'magazine' rather than as a newspaper or periodical, set up its offices in London in 1731. In the ensuing decades, it blossomed.

Meanwhile, those satirists who, thanks to the Licensing Act, were now unable to get their plays staged, turned to a burgeoning new literary form instead. The Licensing Act was *very* good for Fielding in particular. Nobody now reads his stage satires of the 1730s, but in fiction he found that he could comment on contemporary society – and, to a great extent, its political leaders – far more freely than he could on the stage with the Lord Chamberlain breathing down his neck. Fielding subsequently forged a successful career as a novelist, producing *Joseph Andrews* (1742), *Amelia* (1751) and, most famously, *Tom Jones* (1749). He even found time to form the Bow Street Runners, precursors to the Metropolitan Police Force.

The Licensing Act would remain a feature of the British theatre for over two centuries, until the 1960s put paid to it. The decisive moment came in 1968 when a young playwright named Edward Bond wrote a play, *Saved*, featuring a controversial scene in which a group of teenage thugs stone a baby to death. The Lord Chamberlain refused to approve the play for performance, prompting Laurence Olivier to write a letter to the *Observer* in defence of Bond's subject matter. Others joined him, and the Licensing Act was revoked.

# ❧ Defining the Age ❧

A young Samuel Johnson arrived in London in March 1737, a few months before the Licensing Act came into being. His companion was David Garrick, then an unknown young man, who within three years would have a smash-hit play on the London stage, a satire called *Lethe* (which, thanks to the recently introduced censorship, would be a rather tamer affair than Fielding's). Johnson, too, longed to write for the theatre, but his one major attempt at writing drama, *Irene*, met with tepid praise when it was eventually staged. Over the next five decades he would also turn his hand to a novel, *Rasselas*, scores of poems, several influential works of literary criticism and biography, and countless newspaper and magazine articles. But it is for his *Dictionary*, first published in two large volumes in 1755, that Johnson is principally remembered.

Johnson's wasn't the first English dictionary: before his, there had been several such works. Richard Mulcaster had compiled a list of English words in the sixteenth century (albeit without definitions), and in 1604 Robert Cawdrey's *Table Alphabeticall* had appeared. Lexicography is as much about borrowing and improving as about creating from scratch. Johnson's *Dictionary* drew heavily on Nathan Bailey's *A Universal Etymological English Dictionary* (1721), which in turn had relied on John Kersey's *Dictionarium Anglo-Britannicum* (1708), which itself had borrowed generously from John Harris's *An Universal English Dictionary of Arts and Sciences* (1704). But none of these was on the same scale as Samuel Johnson's dictionary. A far greater size and scope would be what Johnson, in 1755, brought to the table – the 'table alphabeticall', that is. It would take him nine years to complete.

Johnson's wasn't even the only dictionary to be published in 1755. In the same year, Scott-Bailey's *A New Universal Etymological English Dictionary* also appeared in London's bookshops.

It is Johnson's dictionary that is remembered in the annals of book history. Why? For one, it was also the first dictionary to use citations for the words it listed, with quotations from Shakespeare, Spenser, Milton, and countless other literary sources. Indeed, part of Johnson's intention in writing the dictionary was to help readers to understand the language of the English literary greats. Another thing in its favour was the (relative) accuracy of its definitions: although Johnson didn't always quite hit the nail on the head, his success rate was a considerable improvement on the work of his precursors. Bailey's *Dictionary*, for instance, had defined 'cat' as 'a creature well known'; 'goat', meanwhile, was 'a beast' and 'strawberry' was described simply as 'a well known fruit'. 'Black' was 'a colour'. 'Penis' was 'a Man's Yard'. You couldn't argue with the factual correctness of such definitions (on the whole), but they did leave a fair bit to be desired. However, Bailey *had* included 'fuck' and 'cunt', two words which would be absent from Johnson's *Dictionary* – and, indeed, from virtually all English dictionaries for another two hundred years, until 1965.

Despite its unparalleled scale, Johnson's dictionary was far from comprehensive, even by mid-eighteenth-century standards. The first edition contained 42,773 entries, a fair number, but it's estimated that there were a good quarter of a million words in the English language even during Johnson's time. Johnson included no words beginning with X, on the basis that 'X begins no word in the English language.' ('Xylophone', in case you were wondering, has only been in print since the mid-nineteenth century.) Still, this was all an improvement on Cawdrey's dictionary of 150 years earlier, which had failed to include any words beginning with W, X or Y. (*Yes*, really!)

The famous definition supplied by Johnson for 'oats' – 'a grain, which in England is generally given to horses, but in Scotland supports the people' – was an old quip when Johnson penned it, and he probably got it from Robert Burton's *The Anatomy of Melancholy*. At any rate, Johnson had his tongue in his cheek when he penned this line: as Henry Hitchings points out in his compelling *Dr. Johnson's Dictionary: The Extraordinary Story of the Book that Defined the World*, when his biographer James Boswell visited Johnson's home town of Lichfield years later, he was surprised to find that Staffordshire oatcakes were a favourite among the locals.

The oft-repeated exchange between Johnson and the ladies searching for improper or indecent words may be a later invention, although it often does the rounds in accounts of the *Dictionary*. The story goes that several cultivated ladies of London society congratulated the great Doctor for having left all indecent words out of his *Dictionary*, to which Johnson retorted, 'Ah, ladies, so you have been looking for them?' But there are several reasons for believing this story to be apocryphal, the chief one being that Johnson did include a few words that would have offended the proprieties of prim eighteenth-century ladies, among them 'bum', 'fart', 'arse', 'piss' and 'turd', though it's true that sexually suggestive words were left out, including even more medical terms like 'penis' and 'vagina' (though, oddly, Johnson does mention the word 'vagina' in his definition for another word).

He also left out 'aardvark', something which Edmund Blackadder would later observe. But, in fairness to Johnson, he could hardly be blamed for this either: the earliest citation for the word is 1785, the year after Johnson died.

# THE AGE OF ROMANTICISM

The 'age of Romanticism' followed the age of Enlightenment, and in many ways responded to it by rejecting many of its guiding principles. Where Enlightenment championed order and reason, Romanticism sought revolution, emotion, imagination and a return to the natural world. Romantics let their hearts, rather than their minds, govern their decisions. As for the idea of governing, the well heeled, well fed and well bred had been in charge for far too long: it was time that the people had a say in how things were done. Liberty, rather than tyranny, was their watchword.

Of course, this is to oversimplify the divide between the two eras, and in many ways there were crossovers: Thomas Paine, the revolutionary writer who shared more with Wordsworth than with Robert Walpole, wrote a book called *The Age of Reason*, championing the rational approach to matters of religion. Romanticism developed the values of the Enlightenment as much as it challenged its emphasis on rationalism and orderliness. But the Romantics certainly moved things forward at a busy time in history.

When did this change of attitude begin? With the storming of the Bastille in 1789, and the start of the French Revolution? Or with that earlier revolution, the American War of Independence, and the signing of the Declaration of Independence in 1776? Or perhaps even earlier than this, when Jean-Jacques Rousseau (of whom more later in this book) published his *Social Contract* in 1762?

Such a quest for 'beginnings' is always fraught with problems. But certainly the spirit of Romanticism – in one sense a (partial) rejection of the search for orderliness that we saw in the previous chapter – seems to have been in place by the 1760s, when three spectacular literary forgeries were unleashed upon an unsuspecting public. All three texts, fakes though they were, signalled the arrival of something new in the world of books, something you probably wouldn't have caught Henry Fielding or Dr Johnson admiring (indeed, Johnson led the attack on one of the forgers, denouncing him as a liar and a fraud). The three forged texts were the 'Ossian' poems, which the Scottish writer James Macpherson claimed to have collected from authentic Gaelic sources (but probably wrote himself); the 'medieval' poems of the fictional fifteenth-century monk Thomas Rowley, which were actually written by an eighteenth-century teenager named Thomas Chatterton; and Horace Walpole's novel *The Castle of Otranto* (of which more shortly). All three counterfeit texts offered a counterblast to the prim and prissy world of scientific classification and intellectual scrutiny which we find in Samuel Johnson's *Dictionary* or Hooke's *Micrographia*. Even Margaret Cavendish would probably have been taken aback.

Although the 'Romantic era' was short-lived in Britain – in the 1830s it would give way to the Victorian period – it had a decisive influence on the world of books, gave us several new genres of fiction, and helped to stoke the fires of not one, but two revolutions. If you have your daffodils at the ready, let's get Romantic.

# ✧ The Gothic Boom ✧

Horace Walpole, who was the son of Sir Robert, gets the credit for writing the first proper Gothic novel. But the odd thing is that, at first, Walpole didn't even put his name to the novel. There was a good reason for this.

Walpole's 1764 book *The Castle of Otranto* was responsible for single-handedly founding the Gothic novel genre (though as I argued in an earlier chapter, aspects of Gothic horror that we now associate with the genre clearly pre-dated Walpole). Walpole claimed the story was a genuine medieval manuscript which had recently been discovered and translated. The literary world flocked to buy this exciting new book. A year later, when the book was reprinted, Walpole added a preface in which he came clean and admitted that he'd made the whole thing up.

In doing so, he founded not only a new literary genre but also one of the perennial features of the Gothic story, the so-called 'found' manuscript. Many of the features of the Gothic that endure today – the subterranean secret, the gloomy castle, the mysterious ghostly sightings – were all there right from the start in Walpole's novel. Without Walpole, it is doubtful whether there could have been any Edgar Allan Poe, *Frankenstein*, *Dracula*, or

Stephen King. This one short novel founded not only a genre but a whole new style of writing.

> Matthew Lewis, known for his 1796 Gothic novel *The Monk*, wrote his will on a servant's hat while dying on board a ship from Jamaica to the UK.

Walpole got the idea for the novel from a dream he had: all he could recall when he woke was 'that I had thought myself in an ancient castle (a very natural dream for a head like mine, filled with Gothic story), and that on the uppermost banister of a great staircase I saw a gigantic hand in armour. In the evening I sat down and began to write, without knowing in the least what I intended to say or relate.' The rest, as they say, is history – or rather decidedly *not* history, but fiction, since the whole thing sprang from Walpole's imagination.

Walpole is credited by the *Oxford English Dictionary* with introducing over 200 new terms into the English language, among them 'beefy', 'malaria', 'nuance', 'sombre', and 'souvenir'. Without doubt his most celebrated neologism was 'serendipity', meaning the 'faculty of making happy and unexpected discoveries by accident'. He coined the word in a letter of 1754, when recounting the 'silly fairy tale' of 'The Three Princes of Serendip' (Serendip was a name for Sri Lanka). The tale is one of the earliest detective stories in existence: it recounts how three princes track down a missing camel largely through luck and good fortune, rather than any forensic skill. 'Serendipity' has been called one of the most difficult words to translate.

Walpole's influence on the Gothic revival extended beyond literature. His London house, Strawberry Hill, was a vast villa that approached the scale and appearance of a castle. Walpole's house became so celebrated that it gave its name not only to an area of London (near Twickenham and lying in the London borough of Richmond), but also to a style of architecture known as Strawberry Hill Gothic.

## Jane Austen's History
❧                                          ❧

Jane Austen famously satirized the Gothic novels of her time in *Northanger Abbey*. Although that novel would not be published until after her death, it was the first of her six novels to be completed, when she was still in her mid-twenties. Indeed, the young Jane Austen's work is fascinating. When she was still a teenager the budding author collected her juvenilia into three hand-bound notebooks. In one of her first stories, 'The Beautiful Cassandra', the heroine (based on Jane's sister) shoplifts a hat and punches a cook.

The most interesting of the three volumes is probably the second, which contains an early attempt at a novel, to which Austen gave the title *Love and Freindship* (*sic*). She would later revise the manuscript into a novel and rename it *Pride and Prejudice*.

But alongside this early draft of *Pride and Prejudice* is a work of non-fiction, *The History of England from the reign of Henry the 4th to the death of Charles the 1st*. Completed in November 1791, it was only first published in 1922, when an edition appeared carrying a preface written by G. K. Chesterton.

The *History*, dedicated to Austen's sister Cassandra, describes its own author as 'a partial, prejudiced, & ignorant Historian', which is more upfront than you'll find most historians being. The title page promises, 'There will be very few Dates in this History.'

The *History*, short though it is, provides a fine early example of the wit and irony that would later become Austen's trademark. There is wry understatement – she mischievously refers to the 'dozen' people martyred for their Protestant faith in the reign of Bloody Mary, when the actual figure was in the hundreds – and Elizabeth I is described as 'that disgrace to humanity, that pest of society'. At such moments, Austen is clearly mocking Elizabeth's detractors. She herself seems quite taken with the Virgin Queen: Gloriana gets more space in the *History* than any other monarch.

The issue of where to place Austen in the history of English literature and culture has been widely discussed. Although most people associate her more with the Georgian, Regency world in which she lived, and point up the associations between her work and that of the eighteenth-century wits like Alexander Pope and Samuel Johnson, she was also writing her mature work – the novels for which she is now principally known – at the height of Romanticism, that artistic movement which challenged many of the older ideas espoused by Pope and his circle.

# The Age of Revolution

The phrase 'pride and prejudice', which would achieve immortality as the title of Jane Austen's most famous novel, was not new when she used it. It turns up three times in rapid succession in Fanny Burney's 1782 novel *Cecilia*, and is also found in two important works that first appeared in 1776, Edward Gibbon's *The Decline and Fall of the Roman Empire* and Thomas Paine's *Common Sense*.

Born in Thetford in Norfolk, Paine (1737–1809) had failed at numerous business ventures before heading across the water to America, where he would play an important role as a pamphleteer stoking the fires of revolution. After his work stirring up rebellion there, Paine would travel to France and support its revolution, at least in the early, less bloody days. His old ally in the American War of Independence, the Irish Whig politician Edmund Burke, opposed the French Revolution and wrote a pamphlet, *Reflections on the Revolution in France* (1790), condemning the actions of the revolutionaries. In response, Paine wrote a pamphlet, *Rights of Man*, published in two volumes in 1791 and 1792, which supported the idea of abolishing the monarchical and aristocratic system in France. Paine did, however, oppose the execution of the king, Louis XVI, and was against capital punishment on principle. This was partly what landed him in trouble – and in prison – in 1793.

Along with *Common Sense* and *Rights of Man*, Paine's other great work and the one that remains his most readable – and his funniest – is *The Age of Reason* (1793–4), the early portions of which were written in his cell in Paris. In *The Age of Reason* Paine subjects the Bible to rigorous scrutiny and criticism. His aim was to show that the Scriptures were not the word of God, but a bunch of man-made texts, by highlighting the inconsistencies and incongruities within the Old and New Testaments. By all means worship God if you wish, Paine says, but don't be thinking that the Bible is God's divine word.

His tone is frequently casual and even flippant. Here he is on the Genesis story of Adam and Eve: 'The Christian Mythologists, after having confined Satan in a pit, were obliged to let him out again to bring on the sequel of the fable. He is then introduced into the Garden of Eden, in the shape of a snake or a serpent, and in that shape he enters into familiar conversation with Eve, who is no way surprised to hear a snake talk; and the issue of this tête-à-tête is that he persuades her to eat an apple, and the eating of that apple damns all mankind.' One can't imagine Milton's *Paradise Lost* packing quite the same punch if it had been phrased in such everyday terms.

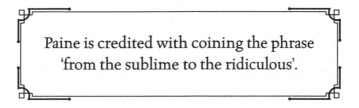

Paine is credited with coining the phrase 'from the sublime to the ridiculous'.

Paine's contemporaries felt that he sometimes went too far in his witty and facetious attitude to biblical stories. For instance, on the fact that the alleged sinner and supposed prostitute Mary Magdalene was the first person to see Jesus after the resurrection, Paine writes: 'she was a woman of a large acquaintance, and it was not an ill conjecture that she might be upon the stroll'. Paine's language at such moments was attacked by many for its 'vulgarity' – that is, for writing in a way that would appeal to both the middle and working classes. But this was very deliberate on his part, an aspect of his egalitarian nature and his desire to reach out to 'the common man'.

One of the most persistent 'charges' laid against Paine is that he was an atheist. In fact, as he makes repeatedly clear in *The Age of Reason*, he was a deist (that is, one who believes in a Creator but not an intervening God) whose aim was to defend God against the (mis)representations of him in the Old and New Testaments. On the contrary, he claimed that he wrote *The Age of Reason* as a counterblast to atheism, which was on the rise in France at the time.

But such intellectual nuances seemed to be beyond the grasp of most of his friends and associates. Only six people attended his funeral when he died in 1809. To this day, nobody knows for sure where his bones lie. He remains a much more valued figure in America than he ever has been in his home country. Yet his influence was considerable. As he remarked in a letter to George Washington in 1789, 'A share in two revolutions is living to some purpose.'

## The First Feminist?

Paine wrote his *Rights of Man* (1791–2) in response to Burke's *Reflections on the Revolution in France* (1790), but another writer also published a 'rights of man' response to Burke. Her name was Mary Wollstonecraft, and her book, published only a few weeks after Burke's, was called *A Vindication of the Rights of Men*. In it, Wollstonecraft argues for republicanism and against aristocracy and hereditary privilege, much as her friend Paine would do. But it is for the follow-up to this work that Wollstonecraft is now celebrated.

Wollstonecraft is chiefly remembered nowadays for doing two

things. The first is for being the mother of Mary Wollstonecraft Godwin, later to become known as Mary Shelley, author of *Frankenstein*. The second is for writing a book called *A Vindication of the Rights of Woman* (1792), a landmark feminist text.

In *A Vindication*, Wollstonecraft argued that women should be better educated, since it was essentially left up to them to educate the next generation. A fuller education would also make them better companions for their husbands. This is close to what Thomas Elyot had advocated some 250 years before, but Wollstonecraft vastly improved upon Elyot's idea. Wollstonecraft also rejected the idea that women are innately less intelligent than men, pointing out that it's the lack of education women receive that's the problem. The book was hugely popular and received favourable reviews in numerous leading periodicals and magazines.

Yet not everyone approved of the arguments put forward in *A Vindication*. Indeed, the adverse responses to Wollstonecraft's book are strikingly similar to the far more recent objections to same-sex marriage. A man named Thomas Taylor anonymously published a spoof response titled *A Vindication of the Rights of Brutes*, extending Wollstonecraft's request to similar equal rights for animals, vegetables, and even 'the most apparently contemptible clod of earth'. (It may be significant here that Taylor had earlier been Wollstonecraft's landlord.) *A Vindication* even got Wollstonecraft branded a 'prostitute': one bishop called her an 'advocate of priapism', because in one of her works she dared to refer to the 'organs of reproduction' (Priapus was the fertility god of Greek myth, usually depicted with a large erection).

Perhaps surprisingly, given that *A Vindication* is now viewed as a work of early feminism, Wollstonecraft was often deeply critical of the women of her time. She had already called for improved education of women in her first book, *Thoughts on the Education of Daughters* (1787), and here returned to the idea. But feminist commentators have since criticized *A Vindication* for the way in which Wollstonecraft appears to mock and belittle the women of her day, and some have even accused her of being a reluctant woman – one who wished, deep down, that she'd been born a man. Yet such criticisms run the risk of overlooking Wollstonecraft's broader point: that a society which deprives most of its women of a sufficient education is inevitably going to keep women out of the intellectual front rank. But *A Vindication* did what it needed to: it stirred up debate on the topic and remains a central work of 'feminist' literature, before the word had even come into being. It was people like Wollstonecraft who helped to ensure that it did.

# The Other Darwin

In the nineteenth century, two men named Darwin published 'origin' books outlining a theory of evolution. The one everyone knows about is Charles Darwin, whose *On the Origin of Species* appeared in 1859, but what is less well known is that his grandfather, Erasmus Darwin, also published a theory of evolution. Originally titled *The Origin of Society*, the book was renamed *The Temple of Nature* and published in 1803.

Erasmus Darwin's achievements were considerable. His medical skill led to an invitation to serve as the king's physician to George III, though Darwin declined the offer. One of his poems, *The Botanic Garden*, anticipates the Big Bang theory when it describes an explosion, a 'mass' which 'starts into a million suns'; this poem also contains the earliest reference to hydrogen in English writing. He was also a restless inventor, devising both a copying machine and a speaking machine to impress his friends, though neither design ever received a patent. He also, it would appear, liked eating. Ever the innovator, he responded to his growing waistline not by going on a diet – such a thing hadn't really caught on yet – but by cutting a hole in his dining table that could accommodate his considerable girth. He was also very active in the Birmingham 'lunar society', a group of local thinkers who met once a month on the night of the full moon, to discuss ideas of political reform (among other things, the society supported the French Revolution until it became too bloody). As well as being the grandfather of Charles Darwin, Erasmus could also name Francis Galton – who would earn notoriety as a leading proponent of eugenics – as his grandson.

One of Erasmus Darwin's poems, *Zoonomia*, introduced the word 'tonsillitis' into the English language.

His literary achievement is noteworthy, too. Wordsworth was a fan of Darwin's poetry, and William Blake – who provided some of the illustrations for Darwin's *The Botanic Garden* – was influenced by him. Shelley borrowed some of the imagery from the book for the opening sections of his *Queen Mab*. It has even been suggested that discussions between Shelley and Byron prompted by Darwin's poem helped to inspire Mary Shelley's *Frankenstein*. Coleridge, however, seems to have been less enamoured: 'I absolutely nauseate Darwin's poem,' he wrote of *The Botanic Garden*. He may have been protesting too much: he, too, appears to have been influenced by Darwin's work.

*The Temple of Nature* was a long poem written in the by then old-fashioned rhyming couplets of Dryden and Pope, but it was an important book in terms of its attention to detail. As with the Romantic poetry of Wordsworth and Coleridge, it celebrates nature and tries to bring man closer to it, though – as Darwin's use of rhyming couplets suggests – the emphasis was on order and classification rather than the more Romantic notions of spontaneity and release. We find it difficult to imagine Erasmus Darwin frolicking among a field of daffodils.

Yet as a popularizer of scientific ideas, Erasmus Darwin was hugely influential on a whole generation – indeed, several generations – of Romantics. His theory of evolution, put forward in *The Temple of Nature*, is somewhat more general than that which his grandson would be able to outline over fifty years later. 'All nature exists in a state of perpetual improvement,' he wrote. But it's more than this. For the very principle that underpins Charles Darwin's later theory of evolution, namely natural selection or 'survival of the fittest', is also part of Erasmus' theory, albeit in less clearly defined terms: 'From Hunger's arms the shafts of Death are hurl'd, / And one great Slaughter-house the warring world!' What Erasmus was missing – namely, hard evidence of how this struggle for existence affected the evolution of different species – his grandson would supply some half a century later.

# ✧ *Frankenstein* ✧

There is a world of difference between Mary Shelley's original 1818 novel *Frankenstein* and the countless films that have been inspired by it. Even Kenneth Branagh's 1994 adaptation, *Mary Shelley's Frankenstein*, adds much to Shelley's original vision and in doing so takes much away. Its title may signal fidelity to the original, but it ends up botching the job on Shelley's book, and has to make desperate attempts to stitch together the disparate pieces to form a coherent, and living, whole. The result is, if not quite a monster, then at least a mess.

But then the book is always accompanied by misreadings or misapprehensions, such as the pedants' favourite topic, the famous conflation of the creator with the (unnamed) creature (so people talk of 'Frankenstein' instead of Frankenstein's monster). Then there is the belief that the creator is 'Doctor Frankenstein' (not so: in the book he is but a humble student). *Frankenstein* is a famous book which everyone knows – or, more precisely, which everyone thinks they know.

Shelley was just a teenager when she began writing it, in 1816. The circumstances of its genesis are well known: in 1815 in Indonesia, the volcano Mount Tambora erupted, blasting so much debris into the upper atmosphere that it caused a drop of around 0.5 degrees Celsius in the average global temperature. This led to a subsequent failure of many crops, with 1816 becoming known as 'The Year Without a Summer' (Byron documented the event in his poem 'Darkness'). Mary Shelley, along with her poet husband, Percy Bysshe, went to stay at Lake Geneva with Byron. To pass the time they told ghost stories to each other, and one of them, Mary Shelley's tale, became the novel *Frankenstein*.

But what is *Frankenstein* really about? It is often cited as a moral fable about the dangers of playing God, of being a sort of modern-day Prometheus – in Greek mythology, he stole fire from the gods and gave it to man (indeed, the novel's subtitle is *The Modern Prometheus*). This is undoubtedly part of the novel's message, but the *creation* of the monster – or, more accurately, the *Creature* – is not what makes the Creature turn against his creator. It is Frankenstein's subsequent rejection of the creature he has made which leads to the creature's violent and destructive behaviour. The novel is not about bad science, but bad parenting.

Shelley would go on to write a number of other novels, including the first post-apocalyptic novel, *The Last Man*, in 1826. She considered that her best book, rather than *Frankenstein*. What's more, although *Frankenstein* was Shelley's first novel, it wasn't the first book she published. In 1817, a year before her most famous novel appeared, Mary Shelley and her husband Percy published *History of a Six Weeks' Tour through a part of France, Switzerland, Germany, and Holland; with Letters Descriptive of a Sail Round the Lake of Geneva and of the Glaciers of Chamouni*. The book was largely Mary's work, meaning that it should take the mantle as her first book, rather than *Frankenstein*.

## ✧ Untrue Blood ✧

Which writer, associated with the Romantic movement, is being described? Born in 1795, he died prematurely in 1821. He was an associate of Shelley and Byron, although the latter had few kind words to say about him. He trained as a doctor, although he became disillusioned with the medical profession.

The above description could apply to John Keats (right down to the birth and death dates – and, memorably, Byron criticized Keats's poetry for being 'mental masturbation'), but in fact it also refers to a relatively forgotten figure, Dr John William Polidori. He was supposedly the youngest-ever person to qualify from Edinburgh medical school, at just twenty years of age, but it's not for his services to medicine that he's remembered. Instead, if he is remembered at all, it is as the author of the first vampire novel.

*The Vampyre* came out of the same ghost-story competition in Geneva that produced Mary Shelley's *Frankenstein*: Polidori was another guest at Byron's villa during that summer of 1816. He was there partly as Byron's travelling companion but also as his doctor, should the poet or any of his guests require urgent medical attention. Polidori's training as a surgeon had brought him into close contact with newly deceased corpses at Edinburgh, home of the most famous double act in the 'resurrection' game, the murderers Burke and Hare. Victor Frankenstein, too, digs up bodies in order to perform scientific experimentation on them. It would appear that *Frankenstein* and *The Vampyre* have more in common than the fact that they were both conceived on the same holiday.

Curiously, though, in the original ghost-story competition, Polidori's tale was somewhat different: according to Mary Shelley his initial story featured a skull-headed lady, took as its focus the witnessing of some indiscretion through a keyhole, and was signally lacking in vampires. Byron was the real originator of the vampiric theme, having sketched out an outline for a vampire story and told it to his physician. (Polidori's original story about the skull-faced lady would later be written up into his novel *Ernestus Berchtold, or the Modern Oedipus* – its subtitle echoing

Shelley's *Frankenstein, or the Modern Prometheus*.)

*The Vampyre* has been called the first vampire novel but might be more accurately described as a novella, given its slimness: the first book edition ran to barely eighty pages. It tells of a young Englishman, Aubrey, who befriends a nobleman, Ruthven, who turns out to be a vampire (so far, so *Dracula* – nearly eighty years before Stoker's novel). The two men tour Europe together, with Ruthven sucking every neck in sight. In the end, he marries Aubrey's own sister, sucking her dry on their wedding night before disappearing, leaving his bride's corpse in his wake. Thus was established the now ubiquitous literary trope of the human–vampire hybrid – often aristocratic, always alluring – who drinks the blood of his victims, not to mention the curious fetishistic blending of sex and romance with blood-drinking. No Polidori, no *Twilight* or *True Blood*. Polidori's vital gift to vampire fiction was to turn the vampire into a sexy Byronic hero: brooding, attractive, and above all, dangerous.

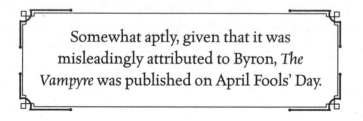

Somewhat aptly, given that it was misleadingly attributed to Byron, *The Vampyre* was published on April Fools' Day.

*The Vampyre* was written hastily, the product of 'two or three idle mornings' according to Polidori himself, and nearly never made it into print at all. It might well have languished forgotten at Byron's villa, if it had been left to Polidori himself (and, one suspects, Byron too). When the good doctor, 'Polly

Dolly' as Byron later nicknamed him, was dismissed from Byron's service later in the summer of 1816, Polidori left Geneva without taking his manuscript with him. Somehow, and precisely how remains a mystery, the story found its way to the London offices of Henry Colburn, editor of the *New Monthly Magazine*, who published the tale in 1819 with Lord Byron credited, mischievously, as the book's author.

In fact, despite his role in originating the general idea for the book, Byron hated and disowned the story, not least because the central character was modelled rather unflatteringly on him. (The name Ruthven was borrowed from the villainous aristocratic hero of Lady Caroline Lamb's novel *Glenarvon*, a scathing and thinly veiled attack on Byron by his former mistress.) Despite the fact that both Byron and Polidori affirmed that Polidori and not Byron was the book's author, many readers continued to view the book as a quintessentially Byronic piece. Goethe even thought it the best thing Byron wrote, apparently happy to overlook the fact that Byron hadn't written it.

*The Vampyre* was a huge success. The 1820s were the decade of the vampire craze: suddenly everyone was sinking their teeth into the genre. There were operatic adaptations of *The Vampyre*, further works of fiction (produced by Alexandre Dumas and Nikolai Gogol, among others), plays, paintings, and other artistic representations. The fictional vampire had been born. However, Polidori died unaware of any of this. In 1821, having failed to achieve any real recognition for his story, he died, probably by his own hand, in obscurity, aged just twenty-five.

# THE VICTORIANS

The reign of Queen Victoria (1837–1901) was a period of dramatic change in Britain, and, for that matter, the world: the Victorian era saw the development of the railways, the arrival of the telegraph and the telephone, and (literally) groundbreaking scientific discoveries in geology and natural history. Thanks to improved education, more people in Britain could read than ever before, and this led to a rise in the sheer amount of printed material that was around. The Victorians were surrounded by the written word wherever they turned. Books were virtually everywhere.

A great deal of what is commonly believed about Victorian society and culture is, at best, only partly true. For one thing, they weren't as prudish about sex as it's often assumed. It's true their literature was fairly tight-lipped about goings-on in the trouser area, but this was partly due to the way that Victorian literature was circulated: many people didn't buy the latest novels but instead borrowed them from their local library. These libraries were generally rather strict about the sort of thing they'd tolerate in the novels they stocked: no sex or swearing, for starters. As a writer, if your novel wouldn't be stocked by a library such as the mighty Mudie's circulating library, your readership, and therefore your earnings, would be dramatically diminished.

Many novels were published in three volumes before they appeared as a single edition, and before that novels were often serialized in monthly instalments in magazines and newspapers. This meant that writers could effectively get paid several times over for the same novel, which kept people like Thomas Hardy happy (until, that is, he tired of the puritanical preachiness levelled at his more daring novels such as *Jude the Obscure*, and gave up writing novels for good). Being able to divide a finished novel up into three chunks was also a good business move for libraries like Mudie's. If you've ever wondered why so many Victorian novels are such whopping doorstoppers, it's partly a canny publishing venture: libraries could effectively lend a copy of the same novel out to three separate borrowers at once, thus tripling their profits. The downside to all this, of course, was that most Victorian fiction is full of children but has nothing to say about how those children got into the world.

Nor did Victorians cover their piano legs because they were sexually suggestive. It was actually the Victorians who scoffed at the Americans for being so prudish, but the Americans didn't do it either. Captain Frederick Marryat, author of the classic children's novel *The Children of the New Forest* (1847), reported in his 1839 *Diary in America* that American women disapproved of the word 'leg' and insisted that 'limb' be used instead. He also 'unearthed' the story about the Americans covering piano legs because they were suggestive of naked human legs – but it seems that the American lady he spoke to was pulling *his* leg, having spied her opportunity to gull a naive English tourist.

That hasn't stopped the myth from being repeated time and time again ever since – not only about the Americans, but about the Victorians too. In fact, the talk of the town in 1890s England was a scandalous sex memoir written by an author known only as 'Walter' – more of his 'secret life' later.

But enough about sex (for now, at least). In the world of Victorian science, myths abound, too. Charles Darwin wasn't the first person to propose a theory of evolution. He wasn't even the first to suggest the idea of 'natural selection'. (A man named William Charles Wells had proposed this same theory in a short speech of 1813 on the origins of different skin colours; this speech was published in 1818 and proposed the idea of natural selection that Darwin would later make famous, though it must be said that Darwin added more than a little to Wells's original hypothesis.) But as we'll see in this chapter, Darwin's book on evolution wasn't even his bestselling book during his lifetime.

This chapter examines such widely held beliefs and looks at some of the books that tell the *real* history of the Victorians – featuring sex, worms, beetles, detectives and more than a few secret lives.

## ☥ The Dickens Christmas ☥

Since Dickens's *A Christmas Carol* was published in December 1843, there have been countless stage, screen and radio adaptations. The first film adaptation was a short silent movie version in 1901, titled *Scrooge; or, Marley's Ghost*. There have been opera and ballet versions, an all-black musical called *Comin' Uptown* (1979), and even a 1973 mime adaptation for the BBC starring Marcel Marceau. The

Muppets, Mickey Mouse and Mr Magoo have all offered their take on this timeless story.

Although it was the first of his five festive books, *A Christmas Carol* wasn't actually the first Christmas story Dickens wrote. It wasn't even the first Christmas *ghost* story Dickens wrote. He'd already written 'The Story of the Goblins Who Stole a Sexton', featuring miserly Gabriel Grub, an inset tale in his first-ever published novel, *The Pickwick Papers* (1836–7). The tale shares many of the narrative features that would turn up a few years later in *A Christmas Carol*: the misanthropic villain, the Christmas Eve setting, the presence of the supernatural, the use of visions which the main character is forced to witness, the focus on poverty and family, and, most importantly, the reforming of the villain into a better person at the close of the story. It's almost as if Dickens plagiarized *A Christmas Carol* – from himself.

Dickens wrote *A Christmas Carol* in six weeks during October and November 1843, and it appeared just in time for Christmas, on 19 December. The book's effect was immediate. Thomas Carlyle, the Scottish historian (whom Dickens greatly admired), went straight out and bought himself a turkey after reading *A Christmas Carol*. The term 'Scrooge' has entered the language as shorthand for a tight-fisted and miserable person. 'Bah! Humbug!' has become a universally recognized catchphrase, although Scrooge only uses it twice in the book.

> A species of snail, *Ba humbugi*, has even been named in honour of Scrooge's well-known phrase.

Dickens was inspired to write *A Christmas Carol* by observing the plight of the poor, who are represented by the Cratchit family in the book. Right from the start it was seen to be a powerful piece of polemic as well as an entertaining and timeless tale. William Makepeace Thackeray – Dickens's main rival at the time – called the book 'a national benefit', while fellow novelist Margaret Oliphant said that although it was 'the apotheosis of turkey and plum pudding', it 'moved us all in those days as if it had been a new gospel'. The book was more or less single-handedly responsible for the tradition of the Christmas Eve ghost story, which remains with us to this day.

Dickens began his series of public readings from his work – the readings which would eventually contribute to his early death at just fifty-eight – with performances of *A Christmas Carol* in the early 1850s. The readings proved exhausting even for a writer with such seemingly boundless energy as Dickens, self-styled 'Sparkler of Albion'. On days when he gave public readings, he couldn't eat much and instead had two tablespoons of rum flavoured with fresh cream for breakfast and a pint of champagne for tea; half an hour before the start of his performance, he would drink a raw egg beaten into a tumbler of sherry (which, if unappetizing, is at least suitably Christmassy).

Despite its phenomenal success, *A Christmas Carol* didn't actually make Dickens much money at first. This was largely down to the high production costs of the book, which resulted in Dickens collecting a mere £230 in profits, less than a quarter of what he'd been expecting. The Christmas books he wrote after *A Christmas Carol* – *The Chimes* and *The Cricket on the Hearth* – brought gladder financial tidings. Indeed, sales outstripped those of *A Christmas Carol*.

The success of the novel didn't single-handedly create, or popularize, the modern idea of Christmas. Dickens himself acknowledged the influence of the American writer Washington Irving on his Christmas writings. But Dickens's book was part of a wider culture which helped to form the modern conception of the Christmas holiday. Queen Victoria and Prince Albert played their part, with Albert in particular importing numerous elements from Germany. The first Christmas cards were also sent in the same year as Dickens's story was published; of the original 1,000 copies of the inaugural Christmas card that were printed, only twelve remain in existence.

## ♦ A Forgotten Sensation ♦

Charles Dickens was a master of the macabre, whether it's in his Christmas ghost stories, in the chilling Gothic gloom of Satis House in *Great Expectations*, or the squalor of London in *Oliver Twist*. But there was another novelist who most people have never heard of, whose books also offered the Victorian public a good helping of horror. At the height of his career, he sold more copies of his work than Dickens, who is widely thought to have been the bestselling novelist of the age.

This forgotten author was George William MacArthur Reynolds, born in Sandwich in Kent in 1814. In many ways, Reynolds was a more 'modern' man than Dickens, in that he seems to belong less to his time and more to our own. A firm atheist at a time when most people in Britain still regularly attended church, and, like Dickens, a strident critic of the British government and a champion of the poor, Reynolds was also a lover of all things Jewish and a fan of Muslim culture (at a time when many of his peers were banging the drum for colonialism and racial prejudice). Reynolds adopted a multicultural attitude to life and art long before the term had been invented. ('Multiculturalism' was first recorded in 1935, in case you were wondering.) In 1848, he supported the revolutions in Europe, especially in Paris, and championed the poor in their struggle for better pay and political representation. He also supported the Chartists, who were calling for electoral reform in Britain.

In other respects, though, Reynolds was more recognizably 'Victorian': in 1840 he became an outspoken campaigner for temperance, having turned up to a temperance meeting drunk, argued with the leader, and been persuaded to become teetotal. Indeed, arguing was something Reynolds appears to have done a great deal of: it was said that one of his publishers, Dicks, was the one person he never fell out with.

At its height, Reynolds's fiction was so popular that during the 1840s, when Dickens's career was already making him one of the first modern celebrities, Reynolds even outsold the author of *The Pickwick Papers*. Indeed, Reynolds had started out as a shameless copyist of Dickens's work: one of Reynolds's early books was *Pickwick Abroad*, which transported Dickens's hugely successful characters to France (copyright laws weren't as established as they now are, so Reynolds appears to have got away with it). Like Dickens, Reynolds also set up his own publication, *Reynolds' Weekly Newspaper*, which first appeared in 1850. It would continue publication in some form or other until 1969, and thus has the distinction of being the longest-running English working-class radical newspaper. Upon his death in 1879, the trade magazine *The Bookseller* described Reynolds as 'the most popular writer of our times'. Yet this modern man and hugely successful novelist has not had the posthumous reputation or readership that Dickens has enjoyed. Why?

Reynolds's most popular work was a long-running serial novel, *The Mysteries of London* (1844–8). For the idea for this serial, Reynolds once again 'borrowed' heavily from another writer: namely, Eugène Sue, whose *The Mysteries of Paris* had sold well across the Channel (in the 1830s Reynolds had lived for several years in France). At the peak of his fame, Reynolds's book sold 40,000 copies a week in penny instalments. In total, a million copies flew off the shelves before it was published in bound volumes.

But something happened to Reynolds's reputation after his death, and for reasons that are almost as mysterious as the 'Mysteries' in his own novels, his posthumous readership didn't just decline, but more or less disappeared altogether.

Undoubtedly this can partly be put down to the ephemeral way in which his novels were published, in throwaway periodicals and newspapers. The subject matter and the style of Reynolds's work probably didn't help, either. Like Dickens, he wrote feverishly fast, but Reynolds was very much an author of his time, reflecting and drawing on what were often modish attitudes whose significance has now been lost. He was a capable writer, but his style can strike modern readers as too overblown, too sensational, without the subtlety that we encounter in his contemporaries, even in Dickens, who was no stranger to sensation himself. Reynolds's work slots firmly into the 'penny dreadful' tradition, produced to satisfy the public's appetite for exciting stories and horrific, suspense-filled narratives published in serial form.

Perhaps modern readers also find Reynolds's social commentary in his novels too intrusive: he was known to 'go off on one' when highlighting the plight of the poor in his fiction, with the story becoming lost in the midst of his impassioned diatribes. While original readers were prepared to countenance such passages – indeed, many positively enjoyed them – they can come across as too preachy and demagogic for modern tastes.

Yet the best of him is still worth reading. Another of his books, *Wagner the Wehr-wolf* (1847), is one of the first treatments of the werewolf in English fiction. It's one of Reynolds's more readable efforts for modern audiences, and still carries the power to appal and entertain.

## ❖ Cooking the Books ❖

In October 1851, a book appeared that bore, on its title page, the comically absurd name of Lady Maria Clutterbuck. The book had already been through a first edition and had proved so popular with readers that a second was printed in time for the Christmas market. The book's popularity would continue well into the decade, running through five editions before 1860.

The book, *What Shall We Have for Dinner?*, was, in fact, not by a lady named Maria Clutterbuck but by a housewife who bore a name far more recognizable to the 1850s public: Dickens. Catherine Dickens, Charles's wife, was its secret author and took her pseudonym from the name of a character she had played in one of her husband's theatrical productions, *Used Up*, in which Charles and Catherine had acted alongside each other at Rockingham Castle in 1851.

The cookbook, at least as we know it, was a reasonably recent phenomenon. Eliza Acton's *Modern Cookery for Private Families* had been a runaway bestseller following its publication in 1845, and within eight years it had already gone through thirteen editions. It was one of the first cookery books to provide lists of ingredients, along with the precise quantities of each. Hard though it is to believe, cookbooks before Acton's had tended to omit this information, even though it's difficult to imagine an effective recipe without them. (Richard II's *Forme of Cury*, needless to say, had not included these details.) Acton's book was also the first such work to include a recipe for Christmas pudding, another sign that the 1840s were the decade in which the modern British Christmas was created.

Catherine Dickens's book, then, was riding the wave of an immensely popular and lucrative new genre: the cookbook aimed at the burgeoning numbers of middle-class Victorians. Although it was just fifty-five pages in length and didn't provide much detail about how to put the listed ingredients together – something of a limitation for a cookbook even then – it featured an impressive number of recipes, forty-nine in all, among them spicier dishes such as salmon curry. Catherine's recipe for cauliflower cheese made with Parmesan (the Dickenses had visited Italy in the 1840s) is also included. Her book includes one of the earliest soufflé recipes in English, made with Gruyère and Parmesan: soufflé was a dish only recently made easy to cook at home, thanks to the invention of closed ranges with temperature controls.

Catherine's was also one of the first English cookery books to order the dishes along the lines of Russian service – that is, dinner served in successive courses rather than in the French 'buffet' style – which would become the preferred way in which the Victorians chose to dine by the end of the century and has remained so ever since. It was not just a culinary but a social shift: when entertaining others at dinner, the gap between courses enabled more opportunities for conversation among the guests. The modern English dinner party had been born.

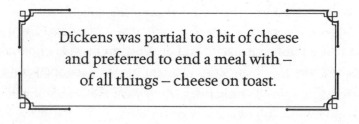

Dickens was partial to a bit of cheese
and preferred to end a meal with –
of all things – cheese on toast.

*What Shall We Have for Dinner?* remained popular until the end of the 1850s, and its popularity might have continued if it hadn't been for the publication, in 1861, of a book that would outsell both Catherine Dickens's book and, for that matter, Eliza Acton's. Titled *Beeton's Book of Household Management*, this new book would represent the last word in cookery – and a fair bit else – for the rest of the Victorian era and beyond. Thereafter, 'Mrs Beeton' would be the byword for Victorian cookery, while Eliza Acton and Lady Maria Clutterbuck would be consigned to relative obscurity in the history of Victorian dining. Catherine, who had acted alongside her husband as Maria Clutterbuck in 1851, had also meanwhile been supplanted in her husband's affections by another actress, Ellen Ternan, and Dickens had separated from Catherine in 1858. But Catherine's one book remains a revealing insight into what mealtimes at the Dickenses' were like. It also sheds light on changing attitudes to dining in nineteenth-century England.

# ✧ The Victorian Internet ✧

Sir Tim Berners-Lee invented the World Wide Web – which is the operating system upon which the internet runs – but what is less well known is that his invention was inspired by a forgotten Victorian bestseller.

*Enquire Within upon Everything* was a 'how-to' miscellany that was first published in 1856, and designed to provide important information on all domestic matters for the Victorian home. Within the first six years of publication it had sold nearly 200,000 copies, and it continued to be reprinted and updated for over a hundred years, until the final edition in 1976. By then, it had been through 126 editions and had sold 1.5 million copies.

The book contained information on a variety of topics: laundry tips, cake recipes, parlour games, first aid, and even (so the editor's introduction proudly informed readers) how to get married and bury a relative (though presumably not on the same day). Other pearls of domestic wisdom included the best way to restore rancid butter (by melting it in a water bath, with some coarsely powdered animal charcoal, before straining it through a flannel, in case you were wondering) and advice to wives (never let your husband find a shirt button missing when he gets dressed for work). The way to avoid a headache, the book recommends, is to keep your feet warm. Gloves, we learn, are always worn by a gentleman while he is out walking, as it's a sign of good breeding. The book's bold claim to contain something about 'everything' was hyperbole, of course, but it cannot be denied that it contained all sorts of things designed to be of use to the average household.

Which brings us to the World Wide Web. In 1980, Tim

Berners-Lee was working at CERN in Switzerland. He was looking into ways of sharing information on local networks and developed a software project which would make this possible. He'd heard of *Enquire Within upon Everything* as a child – which shows how recently it was still to be found in British households – and named his program 'Enquire' in homage to the book, whose title he admired. The 'Enquire' program eventually became the World Wide Web, after Berners-Lee realized that his program could be used to share information more widely than *Enquire* allowed. Berners-Lee could have made himself a very rich man from his invention, but instead he gave the World Wide Web to the world for free.

The name 'World Wide Web', by the way, provides us with another Victorian link. Berners-Lee wasn't the first to use the term, and the *Oxford English Dictionary* provides an example from 1965: it was used in a biography of Charles Darwin to refer to the network of contacts shared by the Victorian naturalist. So, in a weird way, the 'World Wide Web' was always destined to take us back to the Victorians.

## ⟡ Darwin's Bestseller ⟡

Let's talk about worms. There are some 36,000 species of worm, and over 3,000 species of earthworm alone. Many earthworms have ten – yes, *ten* – hearts. South African earthworms have been known to grow to a colossal 22 feet in length. Worms, in short, are fascinating.

It's easy to see, then, why one of the greatest scientific minds of the nineteenth century should have become so interested in them. It's reasonably well known that in 1859 Charles Darwin published *On the Origin of Species*; but it's less widely noted that in 1881 he published *The Formation of Vegetable Mould through the Action of Worms*, the last book to appear before he died. It may sound an unpromising title for a bestseller, but the book outsold *On the Origin of Species* in Darwin's lifetime. Not bad for a book that is essentially about worm-excrement.

The idea of the book came out of a long-standing interest in earthworms. The man who had planted the seed for the book was, oddly, the potter Josiah Wedgwood, who happened to be Darwin's uncle. During 1837, Darwin, who was suffering from a series of maladies that he'd picked up during his voyage on the *Beagle*, from which he'd recently returned, went to visit Wedgwood at his Staffordshire home. Expressing an avuncular interest in his nephew's health, Wedgwood sought something to interest Darwin during his stay. He tentatively suggested earthworms, but thought such a trivial thing would be beneath Darwin's interest. But Darwin was enthralled by the worms and set to work studying them.

'It may be doubted whether there are many other animals which have played so important a part in the history of the world as have these lowly organized creatures,' Darwin declares in *The Formation of Vegetable Mould*. What Darwin's book showed was that, far from being garden pests, earthworms were the life's blood of an average garden: their presence was crucial in helping the soil, aerating it and enabling water to drain away. Worms, Darwin's book revealed, are nature's irrigation system. Having worms in the soil is what makes the growth of many plants possible, too. The idea of worms as nature's unsung heroes obviously caught on with the Victorian reading public, who rushed to buy Darwin's book.

Darwin's book was the culmination of over forty years of research on earthworms – more than *On the Origin of Species*, it was his life's work. He wanted to publish the fruits of his work on worms 'before joining them', as he wryly put it.

# ✥ A Novel Village ✥

The author Charles Kingsley took a keen interest in the scientific developments going on around him and had no problem reconciling his religious faith with Darwin's theory of evolution: Kingsley read a review copy of *On the Origin of Species* in 1859 before it had even been published and became a friend and correspondent of Darwin's in the 1860s. Kingsley's most enduringly popular book, *The Water-Babies* (1863), is about a sort of 'moral evolution' to match its boy hero's own physical evolution (into a water-baby, among other things, but ultimately into a successful and morally upright Victorian gentleman).

*The Water-Babies* has to be one of the oddest children's classics ever written. At once a fantasy novel for children and a Christian moral fable, it also contains lengthy discursive sections on Darwin's theory of evolution and aspects of political satire, as if Kingsley had forgotten who his target readership were. The book tells the story of the boy chimney sweep Tom, who goes beneath the water and becomes a 'water-baby'. In many ways the tale of a child slipping underwater into an alternate world of fantasy, where the Victorian world is curiously inverted, foreshadows that other classic of children's literature produced in the 1860s, Lewis Carroll's *Alice's Adventures in Wonderland*, which appeared just two years after *The Water-Babies*. Both novels feature a child leaving behind the real world for a fantasy world where normal logic and systems are inverted; Kingsley's novel features a lobster (possibly the inspiration for the Lobster Quadrille in Carroll's book) and, curiously, the phrases 'grinning like a Cheshire cat' and 'as mad as a March hare', two creatures who turn up in Carroll's book not as mere similes but as actual characters, as though Carroll had chosen to take Kingsley's book literally. But whereas Carroll eschewed moralizing, Kingsley – who, like Carroll, was a man of the cloth as well as a writer – saw it as his duty to teach children how to lead an ethical life.

But Kingsley's popularity among younger readers extended beyond *The Water-Babies* in his own lifetime, and although not written with children in mind, the Tudor derring-do of one of his earlier novels, *Westward Ho!* (1855), would prove a favourite with Victorian children. The young protagonist of the novel, Amyas Leigh, sets sail for the Caribbean with the privateer who will later be the hero of the Spanish Armada, Francis Drake. They have a series of adventures – including scrapes with England's dread foe, the Spanish. The novel begins in the town of Bideford in Devon, the county that sired not only Drake but also that other great Elizabethan adventurer, Sir Walter Ralegh.

> Devon has given the world the Victorian explorer Sir Richard Burton as well as Scott of the Antarctic. Clearly there's something in the Devon water.

The popularity of *Westward Ho!* lasted well into the twentieth century, and in 1925 it became the first-ever novel to be adapted for BBC radio, though its fame has since been eclipsed by the Devon village to which the novel gave its name. The village is one of only two places in the entire world whose name contains an exclamation mark – the other being the superbly named Saint-Louis-du-Ha! Ha! in Quebec, Canada.

## ✧ The Two Alices ✧

'Lewis Carroll' was really a man named Charles Lutwidge Dodgson, a mathematician at Christ Church, Oxford. As such, he led something of a double life: to the readers of his *Alice* books he was Lewis Carroll, while to the world of mathematics and to his colleagues at the University of Oxford he was (Reverend) Charles Lutwidge Dodgson, a man who formed his pen name by reversing his two forenames ('Charles Lutwidge' became, through some linguistic jiggery-pokery, 'Lewis Carroll').

There is a famous anecdote about Carroll and Queen Victoria. Victoria enjoyed *Alice's Adventures in Wonderland* so much, the story goes, that she promptly requested a first edition of Carroll's next book. Carroll duly sent her a copy of the next book he published – a mathematical work with the exciting title *An Elementary Treatise on Determinants*. Unfortunately, like most good anecdotes, this one is apparently untrue: Carroll, at least, denied it. Such a story does, however, highlight the oddness of Carroll's double life. Despite the radical nature of his nonsense fiction, Carroll – sorry, *Dodgson* – was a conservative mathematician who resented and dismissed many of the new ideas emerging in mathematics during the nineteenth century. Melanie Bayley, writing in the *New Scientist* in 2009, even speculated that *Alice's Adventures in Wonderland* was intended as a scathing satire on radical new ideas in Victorian mathematics.

Alice Liddell is well known to have been the inspiration behind *Alice's Adventures in Wonderland*, but what is less well known is that she *wasn't* the girl who inspired the Alice in the follow-up book, *Through the Looking-Glass*: the 'Alice' in that book's subtitle, *And What Alice Found There*, refers to Carroll's five-year-old cousin, Alice Theodora Raikes. The reason for this was that, by the time he wrote the sequel to the first *Alice* book, Carroll was no longer on speaking terms with the Liddell family. The first *Alice* book came out of a boat trip on 4 July 1862, during which Dodgson regaled Alice – Liddell, that is – with the story. It was Henry Kingsley, brother of Charles, the author of *The Water-Babies*, who convinced Dodgson to publish it.

Carroll identified himself with the Dodo in *Alice's Adventures in Wonderland*, perhaps because of his difficulty in pronouncing his own name ('Do-Do', from Dodgson).

Carroll was a shy man who suffered from a stammer throughout his life and was deaf in one ear, the result of a fever he suffered in childhood. Perhaps this shyness is what led him to invent so many different roles for himself: mathematician, novelist, photographer. There's a bit in *Alice's Adventures in Wonderland* when Alice gets accused by a pigeon of being a serpent. She denies this, but she finds that her confidence has been shaken in *what* she actually is. 'I can see you're trying to invent something!' the pigeon says. 'It's my own invention', as one of the chapter titles to the book has it. Charles Dodgson was always inventing.

## ✧ The First Detective Novel ✧

The credit for writing the first detective novel usually goes to Wilkie Collins for his 1868 book *The Moonstone*. T. S. Eliot thought so, and many have echoed his assessment. However, there are two earlier contenders for that honour, neither of which is as widely read or remembered as *The Moonstone* but which have the advantage of being written before it and being, well, detective novels.

The first of these two precursors to Collins's novel is a work of 1862 called *The Notting Hill Mystery*. Long before the Bank Holiday carnival was set up or Hugh Grant opened a bookshop there, Notting Hill was the setting for an early example of the detective novel, which pips Collins to the post by a whole six years. Written by an unidentified author using the pseudonym 'Charles Felix', *The Notting Hill Mystery* is about a baron suspected of murdering his wife in order to cash in a claim on her life insurance. It featured illustrations from George du Maurier, grandfather of novelist Daphne and a novelist in his own right.

But even *The Notting Hill Mystery* isn't the first English detective novel. That honour should go to a novel written by one of the most successful authors of the 1860s, Mary Elizabeth Braddon, one of the most popular novelists for the new generation of 'railway readers', people who would read fiction on their train commute to and from work. In 1860 a publisher named William Empson brought out her first novel, the sensationally titled *Three Times Dead*. It was largely ignored. But a year later it was reprinted and given the title *The Trail of the Serpent*, and fared considerably better, selling a thousand copies in its first week (much to the irritation of George Eliot, who disliked such 'silly novels'). What is unusual about its publishing history is that, whereas most Victorian novels were serialized first (published in instalments, usually monthly, in a magazine) and then published as whole volumes, *The Trail of the Serpent* actually appeared as a completed book and was then serialized afterwards. This is because a year after the novel was published, in 1862, Braddon became a household name (and a notorious one at that) following the publication of her hugely successful sensation novel, *Lady Audley's Secret*. The *Halfpenny Journal* (subtitled 'a magazine for all who can read') capitalized on Braddon's fame, and the public's appetite for more of her work, and ran the older novel in twenty-eight parts in 1864–5.

A lurid tale involving murder and false identity, *The Trail of the Serpent* qualifies most definitely as a 'detective' novel not only because a crime is placed at the centre of the narrative but because it has a detective, named Peters, investigating that crime. What makes the novel especially interesting, in addition to its little-known right to the title of 'first detective novel', is the fact that this detective is a mute. Already in the annals of English crime fiction, the detective is marked as an outsider, someone who is shut out from mainstream society. Scholars such as Chris Willis and Kate Watson have argued that the novel therefore qualifies most certainly for the title of the earliest detective novel.

But the question of what was the first detective novel depends very much on how you define 'detective'. Sir Edward Bulwer-Lytton's novel *Eugene Aram* features a character who is a detective in all but name, and is endeavouring to solve a crime, and that novel was published in 1832. Interestingly, Braddon's *The Trail of the Serpent* was influenced by Bulwer-Lytton's work – right down to character names and plot devices – so perhaps it is to Bulwer-Lytton that we should look as the true progenitor of the English detective novel. Yet the modern police force and the notion of official crime investigation only came into being in the Victorian era – so it was only then that the detective novel properly arrived on the (crime) scene.

## ✧ A Pestilential Book ✧

Braddon was one of the most popular novelists of her age, but she yearned for the literary acclaim heaped on her contemporaries Anthony Trollope and George Eliot. Both Trollope and Eliot were writing novels firmly in the realist vein, attempting to depict the daily lives of ordinary human beings without resorting to sensationalism. Braddon had few kind words to say about most English realists, disliking 'the deification of the commonplace' which their work displayed, but she was fond of French writers such as Flaubert and sought to attain literary respectability by writing, alternately, a sensation novel to pay the bills and then a more realist novel that would earn her critical acclaim.

But one English realist writer she did admire was George Eliot, who is probably best known for her vast 'study of provincial life', the 1872 novel *Middlemarch*. *Middlemarch* wasn't George Eliot's first major success as a writer, nor should that honour go to her first volume of fiction, the trilogy of stories collected together as *Scenes of Clerical Life* in 1858. The woman who later called herself George Eliot had her first literary success when she was still in her mid-twenties and still known by her birth name Marian Evans: a translation of a work of German scholarship called *Das Leben Jesu, kritisch bearbeitet*. It was published in Britain in 1846 as *The Life of Jesus, Critically Examined*.

Strauss's book – and Marian Evans's translation – was groundbreaking for its time. Like Paine's *The Age of Reason* half a century before, it chipped away at the idea that biblical stories should be taken literally. What evidence was there for the supernatural claims that the New Testament makes? Strauss saw Jesus as a charismatic teacher but not the son of God: the miracles he performs should be read as myth rather than as straight factual events.

These were dangerous claims to be making then, and proved controversial. Marian Evans's translation certainly provoked some extreme reactions. The Earl of Shaftesbury, clearly not a man to mince his words, called it 'the most pestilential book ever vomited out of the jaws of hell'. Evans's own father threatened to throw her out of the house. But it was formative work for the young author to undertake, and when she became George Eliot just over a decade later, we can clearly see the ways in which Strauss's book influenced her own outlook. The story of Jesus may not be true, Eliot reasoned, but it provides some good moral lessons which modern Victorians should embrace: love your neighbour, turn the other cheek, help your fellow human beings. This ethos is there in the three stories that make up Eliot's first work of fiction, *Scenes of Clerical Life*. The religion of doing good, as Thomas Paine had put it, was one which Eliot put at the centre of her work.

Not all of this could be learned from Strauss's book alone, but the young Marian Evans's job translating his *Life of Jesus* was essential training for the woman who became George Eliot. Rationalism and fellow-feeling could coexist. Strauss's German spirit of enquiry married up perfectly with Eliot's own Victorian sense of charity and sympathy.

## ✧ Railway Times ✧

In her 1856 essay 'The Natural History of German Life', George Eliot wrote: 'The word *railways* . . . will probably call up, in the mind of a man who is not highly locomotive, the image either of a "Bradshaw", or of the station with which he is most familiar, or of an indefinite length of tram-road; he will alternate between these three images, which represent his stock of concrete acquaintance with railways.' For the Victorians, the name 'Bradshaw' was more or less synonymous with rail travel, and for good reason.

The advent of the railways transformed Victorians' everyday lives. When Celia Fiennes was travelling around Britain a hundred and fifty years earlier, it had been on horseback, accompanied by servants, and had taken months. Now, anyone who could afford a third-class ticket could hop on the train on their day off and travel virtually anywhere they liked, in a tiny fraction of the time. They could also live miles away from the place where they worked, and commute in every day.

The railways also transformed people's reading habits, as Braddon's successful career highlights. Her novels were just the sort of thing people would read while they were on their way to work on the train. By the 1860s most major railway stations in Britain had a W. H. Smith stall. In 1860 the company founded a circulating library that enabled subscribers to borrow a book at one station and return it (exchanging it for a new book) at another. One could literally read one's way around the country.

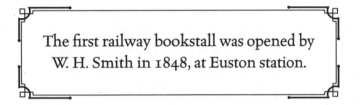

The first railway bookstall was opened by
W. H. Smith in 1848, at Euston station.

But the one book that many railway travellers simply could not be without was their 'Bradshaw'. These railway guides began as simple train timetables but gradually grew into a whole guidebook. In 1841 'Bradshaw' was just eight pages. By 1845 this had quadrupled and by 1898 it was nearly 1,000 pages – a colossal bible for the railway traveller, printed in small type and arranged in double columns, with maps and advertisements, replete with information about the history of cities, towns and villages, as well as tourist hotspots. Hotels were recommended, points of interest noted for the traveller. Other publishers produced railway guides – those of George Samuel Measom were probably Bradshaw's closest rival – but none could match Bradshaw for the scope and the sheer usefulness of the information he provided.

The mid-Victorian era was the age in which people went in search of a secular bible: a single book that would tell them how to negotiate the bewildering and fast-moving world they found developing around them. *Enquire Within upon Everything* ambitiously promised to deliver answers to all the practical questions readers might have, and Mrs Beeton's *Book of Household Management* was another example of a 'how-to' guide. They proved hugely popular. Bradshaw's handbooks were the same: they were *the* book for the modern rail traveller, in an age when the Bible was becoming a less noticeable daily feature of many people's lives.

The arrival of the railways changed the way the Victorians went about their lives in the most fundamental manner possible: it changed their very conception of time. Before the age of steam, different towns and cities around Britain ran on their own local time; the railways changed all that for ever. The introduction of standardized time – which was necessary to ensure smooth running of the trains according to the railway timetable – has even been credited with inspiring a greater degree of punctuality among the population. Railway time became a byword for regularity and precision. The whole country had been brought in line with Greenwich Mean Time by 1880; the Victorian railways had literally invented our modern way of timekeeping.

## ✧ The Bible of Cricket ✧

Say 'Wisden' to most people and they'll think of a vast tome containing charts and tables detailing the results of cricket matches and some 'vital statistics' about the leading players of the game. The first issue of the *Wisden Cricketers' Almanack* would, therefore, come as something of a surprise. Published in 1864, it was just 112 pages long and included the dates of the battles of the English Civil War as well as an account of the trial of King Charles I. It was also padded out with other items of trivia, such as the rules of quoits, the length of Britain's canals, and the results of that year's Oxford–Cambridge boat race. It cost one shilling; these days, you can expect to pay around £20,000 for a copy of this inaugural edition.

Popularly considered 'the Bible of cricket', *Wisden* is the longest-running sports annual in the world. The first issue to exceed 1,000 pages in length was the 1924 edition. Now every new edition tends to be in excess of 1,500 pages. The distinctive yellow jacket – which each new edition of the book now boasts – wasn't a feature from the start, and only became the adopted colour in 1938. Before this, the colour of the book's cover had varied, between yellow, buff, and salmon pink.

John Wisden took relatively early retirement from cricket at the age of thirty-seven, as a result of rheumatism. It was a blow to a successful cricketing career: he was widely considered to be the best all-rounder of his generation. He had a small business selling cricketing equipment, but a friend suggested that Wisden should compile a miscellany outlining all of the most impressive sporting records from the world of cricket – at least, so the story goes. Wisden had himself taken all ten wickets of the opposing team in an 1850 match that pitted the North of England against the South.

Unfortunately, once Wisden embarked on the task of compiling his first cricketing almanac he realized that he hadn't the first idea of what to put in it, so he started to fill out the pages with any interesting trivia that came to hand, which is why, oddly, you can read a discussion of the implications of the death of King Charles I in the very first edition.

In 1913 John Wisden was posthumously awarded Cricketer of the Year in the almanac that proudly bears his name, nearly thirty years after his death and almost half a century after he launched the annual publication that still sells around 40,000 copies each year. But 1864 was the year it all began, and it was a significant year in the development of English cricket. Seven of the first-class county cricket teams came into existence in 1864, while a sixteen-year-old named W. G. Grace – yet to grow his distinctive beard – made his debut at the Oval.

## ✤ Sherlock's Brush with Oblivion ✤

Sir Arthur Ignatius Conan Doyle is best known as a writer, but his achievements were many and varied. He was a keen cricketer and played in ten matches for the Marylebone Cricket Club or MCC. The highlight of his cricketing 'career' was undoubtedly the match in which Doyle managed to take a first-class wicket – the batsman being none other than cricketing legend W. G. Grace. One of his early forays into fiction helped to create the modern mystery surrounding the abandoned ship the *Mary Celeste*, with many newspapers taking his fictional 'statement' – published anonymously in 1884 – as fact. He wrote science fiction, horror stories and historical novels. His legal campaigning led to the establishment of the UK Court of Criminal Appeal. He even applied the methods of logical induction (strictly *not* deduction) employed by his most famous literary creation in order to attempt a solution to the real-life Jack the Ripper case.

But all such achievements have been overshadowed by his most enduring creation: Sherlock Holmes. One of the most recognizable fictional characters ever created, Holmes was – as Martin Booth remarks in his book about Conan Doyle's creation, *The Doctor and the Detective* – as well known as Queen Victoria and considerably more famous than most politicians. Indeed, Holmes came to appear *more* real than actual people, to many readers and fans. When Conan Doyle killed off Holmes in a short story of 1893, one reader wrote to him, 'You brute!' Twenty thousand people cancelled their subscription to *The Strand*, the magazine which published the Sherlock Holmes stories. There were even rumours that people walked about London wearing black armbands, in mourning for the detective. Ten years later, by popular demand, Conan Doyle brought Holmes back from the dead.

Most people would probably argue that two early Sherlock Holmes books were the most important in the 'canon': *A Study in Scarlet* was the first-ever outing for the detective, while *The Adventures of Sherlock Holmes* was the volume of short stories that made Sherlock Holmes a household name. But there is a third book which is arguably more important than either of these. The fact that it was written at all meant that the rest of the detective's adventures – including the popular novel *The Hound of the Baskervilles* and all of the short stories – would be written. Without this other book, *The Sign of the Four* (1890), the detective might have been a one-off character and *A Study in Scarlet* his one and only case.

> A *Study in Scarlet* (1887) was written by Doyle
> in just three weeks while he was running a
> struggling doctor's surgery in Portsmouth.

This is because the first Sherlock Holmes novel was only a mild success. *A Study in Scarlet* (1887) was rejected by many publishers and eventually published in *Beeton's Christmas Annual* (named after the husband of Mrs Beeton, of the book of cookery and household management). Sales were moderate, but it's fair to say the novel didn't take the publishing world by storm.

That might well have been it, had it not been for an influential admirer of *A Study in Scarlet* and a timely dinner party with Oscar Wilde. One person who had read and enjoyed the first novel was the editor Joseph Stoddart, who edited *Lippincott's Monthly Magazine*. Over dinner in 1889, he convinced Doyle to write a second novel featuring the detective, for serialization in the magazine. Wilde, who was also present, agreed to write a novel for the magazine – his only novel, *The Picture of Dorian Gray*. *The Sign of the Four* came to the attention of the editor of the *Strand* magazine, who thought that the detective would make a good character for a series of short stories, and the rest, as we like to say, is history.

But history, of course, has become myth when it comes to Sherlock Holmes. The famous image of Holmes wearing a deerstalker hat is a product of the celebrated images that accompanied the short stories. It was when the *Strand* stories began to appear that Sherlock Holmes became a worldwide sensation. Sidney Paget, who drew the illustrations, had Holmes wearing a deerstalker when the detective went into the country to investigate mysteries at country houses and in small rural villages – never when he was in London – but most people think of the detective as always donning the hat when off to investigate a case.

Curiously, the man who, after Conan Doyle, probably did more than anyone else to create our idea of the great detective got the job illustrating the Sherlock Holmes stories by accident: Sidney Paget only became the illustrator because of a clerical error. The publishers had meant to hire his younger brother, Walter, but they inadvertently addressed the letter to the wrong brother. It turned out to be one of the most serendipitous mistakes in the world of literary illustration.

## ✦ A Handbag? ✦

At that momentous literary dinner in 1889, when Conan Doyle agreed to write a follow-up to *A Study in Scarlet* and Wilde devised *The Picture of Dorian Gray*, two great figures of the 1890s met. But Wilde would go on, of course, to become more famous as a playwright than a novelist, and more famous still for – well, for being Oscar Wilde.

Wilde first came to the world's notice by being effectively one of the first modern celebrities – famous for *being*, rather than for doing anything in particular – but his plays have nevertheless stood the test of time. How many other Victorian playwrights can anyone name? His most famous play is *The Importance of*

*Being Earnest*, staged shortly before his downfall and subsequent imprisonment in 1895.

Although Wilde was undoubtedly homosexual (the term came into being pretty much at the same time he discovered his own same-sex desire) he was, nevertheless, a married man with two sons, for whom he would dream up stories (collected in *The Happy Prince and Other Tales* and *A House of Pomegranates*). He and his wife, Constance Lloyd, were married in 1884; Wilde had earlier unsuccessfully sought the hand of Florence Balcombe, who chose instead to marry Abraham 'Bram' Stoker, who was to become famous as the author of *Dracula*.

But Wilde would later start a double life – the sort that the Victorians, who loved *Strange Case of Dr Jekyll and Mr Hyde*, were so fascinated by – involving rent boys, young male admirers, and, most famously, Lord Alfred Douglas, who came up with the line 'the love that dare not speak its name' to describe his and Wilde's mutual attraction. This double life is played out in the farcical comedy of *The Importance of Being Earnest*, though few members of the original audience would have picked up on the play's origins in Wilde's own life. It sees the two male leads in the play, Jack Worthing and Algernon Moncrieff, inventing excuses to leave their boring everyday lives behind for days on end in order to spend time elsewhere, engaged in the pursuit of pleasure. Their duplicity eventually gets found out, much as Wilde's double life would shortly catch up with him in 1895, the same year that *The Importance of Being Earnest* was charming London theatregoers. The play in performance is known for the two-word comic line 'A handbag?', delivered by Lady Bracknell in response to learning that Jack Worthing was left, as a newborn baby, in a handbag at London Victoria railway station.

(This is thanks to Dame Edith Evans's memorable delivery of the line in a celebrated stage production and, later, the 1952 film adaptation.) In 2007, a first edition of *The Importance of Being Earnest* was donated to a charity shop in Nantwich in England. Aptly, it was placed in a handbag.

## ✧ The Other *Dracula* ✧

In 1897, fans of Gothic fiction were lapping up one novel with especial eagerness. Set among the dark, smoggy streets of contemporary London, the novel features a mysterious foreign figure from the East who is possessed of supernatural powers and newly arrived in the nation's capital. The novel, told from multiple character perspectives, cleverly taps into late Victorian fears and anxieties concerning a host of themes including the British Empire, homosexuality, scientific discoveries, and crime within the metropolis. The book's first print run very quickly sold out, and it remained popular, being made into a film as early as 1919.

The above paragraph is not a description of Bram Stoker's *Dracula* but a summary of the little-known novel which outsold it, at least at the time. *Dracula* was not an initial success. This was surprising in many ways, since Stoker – a theatrical impresario as well as a writer – went to considerable lengths to promote the book. He put on a stage adaptation of the novel in May 1897, a couple of weeks before the book was even published. Reviews were good, too, with the *Daily Mail* lauding Stoker as superior to Mary Shelley and Edgar Allan Poe in the annals of horror fiction. But despite all this the book's sales were average and nothing special. It was popular enough to be reprinted, but initially it was another novel, called *The Beetle*, which was the real horror sensation of the late 1890s.

In early drafts of Bram Stoker's novel, Dracula was originally named 'Count Wampyr'.

*The Beetle*, written by Richard Bernard Heldmann under the pseudonym Richard Marsh, is a quintessentially late-Victorian Gothic horror novel. Like the London in which Sherlock Holmes moved, the world of *The Beetle* is all fog and hansom cabs, with unsavoury figures seemingly lurking in the dark spaces between the lamp posts. The novel touches upon something that *Dracula* and the Sherlock Holmes stories also tap into: the notion of London as a foggy den of vice, crime, and unspeakable horrors. This view of London had also become entrenched in the London consciousness in 1888 by the Jack the Ripper murders, but it was there already, in books such as Robert Louis Stevenson's *Strange Case of Dr Jekyll and Mr Hyde* from 1886.

Why is *The Beetle* not mentioned in the same breath as Stoker's novel, or Stevenson's? Partly it may be Marsh's relative lack of interest in the deeper motivations of his characters. But what the novel lacks in psychological depth it more than makes up for in rip-roaring, page-turning plot. What may also have helped its popularity is the fact that the central target of the novel's titular monster is a British MP. The Victorians evidently enjoyed the idea of a Member of Parliament getting his comeuppance. Indeed, the mystery at the heart of *The Beetle*, not to give too much away, concerns something found in many of the Sherlock Holmes stories: revenge for some crime carried out elsewhere in the British Empire, and a character's past wrongs catching up with him.

*The Beetle* was the zenith of Marsh's popularity: try as he might (and try he certainly did: he published eight novels in 1900 alone), he never managed to match its success in his later work. Marsh may have been forgotten by the mid-twentieth century, but his legacy survived in the form of a famous grandson, Robert Aickman, who became one of the most acclaimed horror writers of his day.

## ✦ A Secret Life ✦

In 1888, London found itself faced with a mystery: a case of secret identity. Who was this man, doing things to women – most of them prostitutes – and how did he come to have such detailed anatomical knowledge? He was known simply by an alias, and his true identity remained unknown – indeed, remains so, despite several theories. But this description doesn't just apply to the shocking and horrific 'Jack the Ripper' murders. For in 1888, the same year as the Ripper was terrorizing London, a scandalous book appeared, which told a different story from your run-of-the-mill Victorian novel.

*My Secret Life*, by an author known simply as 'Walter', was a racy and very explicit account of a Victorian man's sexual exploits. Sex is found on almost every page. You won't find much bonking going on in Dickens, despite the fact that children are everywhere in the Dickensian world. Where do they all come from? Those dresses and waistcoats remain firmly buttoned up, thanks to the restrictions laid down by Mudie's and other influential circulating libraries. Such censorship is partly what led to Thomas Hardy giving up fiction-writing in the mid-1890s. It's even arguably what his 1891 novel *Tess of the d'Urbervilles* is about: lack of frankness about the realities of sex and what some men will do to get their end away.

'Walter', whoever he was, could never be accused of being coy around the beast with two backs. Numerous four-letter words are peppered throughout his account of his carnal adventures like gaudy seasoning. The presence of such words in a book would have led to the immediate prosecution of any publisher who dared to print it, so *My Secret Life* was printed in Amsterdam and then smuggled into Britain. Between 1888 and 1894, eleven volumes comprising over a million words were printed, making *My Secret Life* the pornographic equivalent of *War and Peace*. Indeed, it makes even *War and Peace* look like a slim novella by comparison.

And *My Secret Life* is probably more a 'novel' than it is a true memoir, for all of its ostensible claims to factuality. Who wrote it? Many scholars pin their money on Henry Spencer Ashbee (1834–1900), a book-collector whose other great service to Victorian scholarship was to compile a three-volume bibliography of erotic literature. What mainstream Victorian novelists could only hint at through innuendo, Ashbee addressed directly. Victorian literature is full of sexual hints, the sort of puns that would have young men in the know sniggering to themselves: Charley Bates in *Oliver Twist*, for instance, is known throughout the novel as 'Master Bates'. Anthony Trollope, perhaps aware that his own name was ripe with sexual potential, even names a firm of lawyers in his novel *The Warden* 'Cox and Cumming'. But detailed descriptions of the sexual act were left up to 'Walter' – or Ashbee, if he was indeed the author – to describe.

It would not be until 1995, over a century after the final volume had originally appeared in print, that a British reader or 'gentleman's special interest' enthusiast could legally and easily get hold of a copy of *My Secret Life*. It's never going to have as many readers as *David Copperfield*, but it's valuable for showing the other side of Victorian literature – the side that you couldn't find adorning the shelves in Mudie's or on the railway stalls of W. H. Smith.

# THE AMERICANS

The first Bible printed in America, in 1663, was in the Algonquin language. I open with this fact not just because it is a good fact (though I think it is) but because it reminds us that, right from the beginning, there was something different about the American literary tradition, about the kinds of books they produced. Its status as a new country – as distinct from the 'Old World' of Europe – meant that it required a new way of writing that would take into account its sense of being at the forefront of political, social and literary developments. This sense of newness only heightened following the signing of the Declaration of Independence in 1776 and the founding of the United States as a nation. In the ensuing decades, writers of all kinds would declare their own independence from older literary styles, finding instead new ways to write about their new country and the people in it.

This is neatly exemplified by the notion of the 'Great American Novel': that grand statement in fiction that would sum up the United States and what characterized it, a form of modern national epic. Some commentators say that the definitive

Great American Novel remains to be written; others point to such works as Herman Melville's *Moby-Dick* in the nineteenth century or F. Scott Fitzgerald's *The Great Gatsby* in the twentieth. This chapter is not concerned with Great American Novels, but with lesser-known ones – along with volumes of poetry, eccentric memoirs, modern folk tales, biblical epics, and even books about molluscs. But in some small way they all reflect the development of the United States since its early colonial days – indeed, before there were 'States' to 'Unite' – and the sorts of things that some of the most famous writers in American history have thought worthy subjects for their pens. Whether they reflect the American Dream or something slightly less dreamy or desirable depends on the individual book, but they showcase the evolution of modern America from its infancy to its latter-day status as major world power. So, if you care to know why Louisa May Alcott tried to ban *Huckleberry Finn*, or what connects Washington Irving with women's underwear, read on.

## ✧ The Tenth Muse ✧

In 1666, a great fire consumed much of the considerable library of books owned by the poet Anne Bradstreet. This happened in July – two months before that other great fire that would destroy much of London and that John Evelyn would chronicle in his diary – and it occurred on the other side of the Atlantic. Although she had been born in England in 1612, by the 1660s Bradstreet was living in Andover, Massachusetts, and had made her name as a poet – in fact, she was the first person in America to have a volume of poems published.

Bradstreet could claim descent from such a notable figure as Queen Elizabeth's favourite, Robert Dudley, Earl of Leicester. In 1630, just ten years after the Pilgrim Fathers sailed from England to the New World on the *Mayflower*, Anne and her husband left behind Boston, England, and travelled across the Atlantic on the *Arbella* to establish a new settlement in Massachusetts. They named it after the English town they had left behind, and thus the city of Boston was founded. Later that year, the Bradstreets moved a few miles north of Boston and settled 'the newe towne', later named Cambridge, where Harvard University would be founded a few years later.

> Bradstreet could claim descent from the Elizabethan statesman and poet Sir Philip Sidney, whose work would influence her own.

It was not exactly an environment conducive to poetic creativity. Early colonial life was hard – the life expectancy was not particularly high – and the early settlers in America could afford to take few books with them. As Robert P. Ellis has put it, 'Few poets can have learned their craft under more trying conditions.' Yet learn it she did. Her brother-in-law, travelling back to England in the late 1640s, took a bundle of her poems with him, and they were published in London in 1650 – supposedly without their author's consent – under the title *The Tenth Muse Lately Sprung Up in America*. No woman since Sappho had been so garlanded with the title.

With the appearance of *The Tenth Muse* in 1650, Bradstreet became not only the first published poet from the New World but one of the first female poets from anywhere to have a full book of poems published. An edition published posthumously in 1678 added a number of new poems, which were also noteworthy for being explicitly about married love, not a usual topic for poetry at the time. The poems are a reminder of how hard life was for the early New World settlers: many of Bradstreet's poems are entreaties to God to be allowed to recover from a fever, for the restoration of her husband from 'a burning Ague', or to be delivered from a fit of fainting. But Bradstreet appears to have been a patient sufferer of life's hardships. It's noteworthy that one of the earliest uses of the phrase 'easy come, easy go' appears in *The Tenth Muse*: 'For that which easily comes, as freely goes'.

What marks Bradstreet out from many of her contemporaries is her frankness. In a letter she wrote to her children, she confessed that when she was a teenage girl she experienced 'carnal' desires, vanity, and a faltering in her religious faith. What is also noteworthy is the fact that her poems *are* hers: unlike many previous English women writers, such as Joanna Lumley and Mary Sidney, Bradstreet writes about her own life rather than translating the words of men. She wrote poems addressed to her father, her husband, her children. She wrote about herself and about the life of her fellow colonists in Massachusetts. Although she can hardly be called a confessional poet, it is significant that in the 1950s, three centuries after the publication of *The Tenth Muse*, the leading American confessional poet John Berryman wrote a long and sincere *Homage to Mistress Bradstreet*.

Bradstreet's reputation endured for about thirty years after her death in 1672, with Cotton Mather praising her in 1702, but thereafter she more or less disappears completely from the American consciousness for an entire century. Her name remains more obscure than it deserves to be, although in the last century her reputation has recovered a little. Among those who have claimed descent from Anne Bradstreet are President Herbert Hoover, both Oliver Wendell Holmeses and, more recently, the politician and would-be President John Kerry. Politics, not poetry, has dominated the lives of her more famous descendants.

## ⟡ The Newburyport Nut ⟡

Malden in Massachusetts was settled by Puritans in 1640, shortly after Bradstreet and her family were founding Cambridge. It was in Malden, just a few miles away from Cambridge, that one of the most eccentric characters ever to grace American letters would be born a century later, in the 1740s.

Timothy Dexter often gets overlooked in the annals of literary eccentrics. Known as the 'Newburyport Nut', he was born into a poor family and would later style himself 'Lord' Timothy Dexter, though he appears to have been alone in regarding himself as such. A shrewd businessman, Dexter rose up from his humble origins to amass a small fortune through various canny ventures – marrying a wealthy widow being perhaps the canniest of all. (He would later fake his own death and take his wife to task with a cane for not displaying enough grief at the mock funeral held in his honour.) His wife's money allowed Dexter to fund a whole host of madcap schemes: one of his most lucrative activities was importing wild stray cats into the Caribbean to act as pest-control; this feline enterprise proved more successful than Defoe's cat-themed business forays had done a century before. He succeeded in doing the proverbially impossible – shipping coal to Newcastle (it was during a miners' strike) – and he even managed to convince many people in the West Indies to buy his ladles. They were, in reality, warming pans.

But what he possessed in business sense he lacked in conventional intellect. It was said he bought books he couldn't read. He told the locals of Newburyport in Massachusetts, where he lived, that his wife had died and the woman seen roaming his house was her ghost – which would have been news to his wife, still very much alive as she was. But he possessed a swaggering confidence and self-belief that made him a force to be reckoned with. He had a statue of himself made and inscribed it: 'I am the first in the East, the first in the West and the greatest philosopher in the Western World.' Not many would agree with any of these self-assessments, but many admired his pluck. Three thousand people turned out for his funeral – or rather, his mock funeral. In 1800, that was half the entire population of Newburyport.

But it was in money itself that Dexter made a real fortune – specifically, in old American currency devalued after the American War of Independence. In 1802 he published a book about his success, *A Pickle for the Knowing Ones*, that contained no punctuation. In later editions, he printed a list of punctuation marks and advised readers to add their own, as if it were a matter of lightly seasoning the text with a few commas and colons here and there. The book was also riddled with misspelled words and generally difficult to follow.

The first sentence gives a sense of its, well, lack of sense:

> Ime the first Lord in the younited States of A mercury
> now of Newburyport it is the voise of the peopel and I
> cant Help it and so Let it goue Now as I must be Lord
> there will foller many more Lords pretty soune for it
> Dont hurt A Cat Nor the mouse Nor the son Nor the
> water Nor the Eare

The Lord alone knows what that means – Lord Dexter, that is. I say 'first sentence' but of course, really, the whole book is the first sentence, as there aren't any full stops.

Subtitled *Plain Truths in a Homespun Dress*, the book was not just about Dexter's life but his opinions about everything from religion and contemporary politics to his own wife. Dexter earns his place in this list less for his literary merit than for his larger-than-life embodiment of the American enterprising spirit, later to be represented by a writer like Mark Twain (who possessed more literary skill but was a far less successful businessman than Dexter). But the same spirit of innovation and self-confidence that we find in his business dealings can be observed in the curious short book he wrote. He simply didn't *care* that his book broke with convention and decided to forgo traditional (or indeed any) punctuation. Before later nineteenth-century American writers such as Walt Whitman and Emily Dickinson invented a new poetic style that could be considered recognizably American, Dexter declared his country's literary independence in prose with *A Pickle for the Knowing Ones*. It was not much of a start in literary terms, but it was a start, nonetheless.

## ❖ America's First Writer ❖

Washington Irving has a claim to being the first truly great American writer. Born in 1783, he was named after one of the heroes of the American War of Independence that had made Timothy Dexter so rich. That war hero, George Washington, went on to become the first official President of the newly formed United States of America in 1789. Irving was born in New York and would help to put the city on the literary map.

Indeed, Irving's first book was a humorous history of New York, which proved a huge success. *Knickerbocker's History of New York* (1809) was so popular that 'Knickerbocker', from Irving's fictional creation Diedrich Knickerbocker, came to be used as a name for an inhabitant of New York; it would also, in time, give its name to the ice-cream sundae known as the Knickerbocker Glory. Further down the line, it also gave us the word 'knickers' as a term for women's underwear. 'Knickers' has never been out of use since.

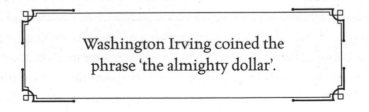

Washington Irving coined the
phrase 'the almighty dollar'.

Irving helped to create many other aspects of New York's mythology, giving this new city and state a sense of history and identity. In 1807 he was the first person to refer to New York as 'Gotham City', in the satirical periodical *Salmagundi*. Irving borrowed the name from the Nottinghamshire village in England, which was reputedly inhabited by fools. (This legend itself derived from medieval times, and the tale of the 'Wise Men of Gotham': the story goes that in the thirteenth century, King John wanted to build a hunting lodge near the village, but decided against it because the people of the village appeared to be a bit simple. Whenever the king's men arrived they found villagers doing incredibly stupid things: attempting to drown eels, or rolling cheeses down a hill in the hope that they'd find their way to the Nottingham fair. John promptly moved his lodge elsewhere.) Of course, since Irving first coined the name 'Gotham', the Batman comic strip and films have cemented the phrase 'Gotham City' firmly in the American – and, indeed, the world's – psyche.

The two stories of Irving's which remain widely enjoyed are the tales of Rip Van Winkle and Sleepy Hollow – modern legends for a new nation. These both appeared in *The Sketch Book of Geoffrey Crayon, Gent.* (1819–20). 'Rip Van Winkle', the story of the man who goes to sleep in the Catskill Mountains and wakes up twenty years later to find his wife dead and his son grown up, was written by Irving while he was staying in England, in 1819. 'The Legend of Sleepy Hollow', written a year later, has become a Halloween classic. Curiously, the author who gave us these two somnolent titles suffered from insomnia: perhaps his fiction was a way of living out the good night's sleep that Irving himself could only dream of – *day*dream of, that is.

Irving also helped to create the modern idea of Christmas. Charles Dickens often gets the credit for inventing our notion of Christmas, with goodwill to everyone, the resurrection of old and formerly outdated customs, and the big Christmas feast. It's certainly true that before the early nineteenth century, the older Christmas celebrations of the Middle Ages were on the wane, but it was not Dickens who first began to popularize them again. He himself was greatly influenced by Irving. Indeed, the anonymously published 1823 poem 'A Visit from St Nicholas' (also known as ''Twas the night before Christmas') also gets the credit for inventing the myth of Santa Claus with his flying sleigh and reindeer, but Irving was ahead of this poem, too: in 1812 he added passages to his revised *Knickerbocker's History of New York* which helped to foster this renewed interest in the idea of Santa Claus. Like Dickens, he wrote five Christmas stories, and, like Dickens also, he championed traditional festive customs which had fallen out of favour (and which he had experienced while staying in England). So next time you're sipping your eggnog round a festive fire, raise your glass in a toast to Irving, the man who helped to invent Christmas as we know it.

## ♦ Poe's Molluscs ♦

Ask Edgar Allan Poe aficionados for the title of their favourite book by him and a few suggestions might readily spring to mind: *Tamerlane and Other Poems*, his first book, a first edition of which is rare and highly prized; *Tales of the Grotesque and Arabesque*, featuring some of his classic stories such as 'The Fall of the House of Usher'; or perhaps *The Raven and Other Poems*, for that volume's title poem and Halloween favourite. What even the diehard Poe fan is unlikely to answer, though, is *The Conchologist's First Book: or, A System of Testaceous Malacology, arranged Expressly for the Use of Schools.*

For a start, the title doesn't exactly sound like a winner.

Yet it was this little-known book of testaceous malacology – molluscs with shells, to the rest of us – which proved the most popular of Poe's books during his lifetime. It was the only one popular enough to be reprinted. First published in 1839, it went through further editions in 1840 and 1845. By the time Poe died in 1849, it was the one unequivocal bestseller of his career. Snails, it turns out, sell.

How Poe came to write a book on molluscs is curious. A friend of his, Thomas Wyatt, had written a book on the subject, published in 1838. Unfortunately, owing to its high price, barely a copy was sold. Wyatt wanted to make money from his molluscs, but the expensive edition his publishers had put out was hardly likely to trouble the bestseller lists. In order to get round this problem, he arranged to publish an abridged cheap edition of his book with a different publisher and a different author's name on the title page. This is where Poe enters the story. Poe made very little money from his short stories and poems, even though he was helping to invent the modern literary genres of the detective story and science fiction, to say nothing of his contribution to the horror genre. So a bit of extra cash for what would be quite a small amount of work seemed like a good deal. Poe was paid fifty dollars for his role in editing, and taking the credit for, this cut-price version of Wyatt's shells book.

Most of Poe's biographers describe *The Conchologist's First Book* in one word: 'hackwork'. Stephen Jay Gould, in *Dinosaur in a Haystack*, gave Poe's shells less short shrift, seeing *The Conchologist's First Book* – and Poe's contribution to it – as an important work of popular natural history. For one thing, the book was innovative in that it treated not just the shells but the molluscs the shells belonged to. Most studies of conchology produced until this point – including the two that Poe liberally borrowed from – tended to focus on the shells and pay the creatures who produced these outer husks scant attention. Poe discussed the molluscs as well as their exterior casings. As far as we know, this was his idea, suggesting that although he knew little about the subject, he knew how to package the information in a way that would appeal to the layperson. Taking much of the required material from the French anatomist Georges Cuvier, Poe created a new kind of book which saw the mollusc and its shell as a coherent entity that needed to be understood together. It may not be sitting on the bookshelf of many Poe fans, not even his most ardent admirers, but it showcases his extraordinary ability to synthesize various influences in order to form something influential and new. As with his science fiction and his detective stories, *The Conchologist's First Book* is an example of Poe's enterprising innovation.

## ✧ An April Fools' Book ✧

*Moby-Dick* is now hailed as one of the greatest of American novels, but it was not always thus: the book certainly signalled a change in its author's fortunes, but not of the good kind. Herman Melville had been critically and commercially successful during the early years of his career, when his novels *Typee* and *Omoo* offered high adventure in the South Seas. The American public gratefully devoured them. *Moby-Dick* offered something altogether different, and met with hostile reviews when it first appeared. Melville's career never recovered from its poor reception, and he slid into obscurity in later life. It was only in the twentieth century, and particularly in the wake of literary modernism, that Melville's work was rediscovered and truly appreciated.

> Between 1863 and 1887, an average of twenty-three copies of *Moby-Dick* were sold each year. It now sells more copies each year than were sold in the entire nineteenth century.

And so it was that his later novel *The Confidence-Man* (1857) was virtually ignored upon publication, and even now is little-known outside Melville's diehard fan base. Like a number of subsequent novels, from James Joyce's *Ulysses* to Virginia Woolf's *Mrs Dalloway* to Ian McEwan's *Saturday*, the action takes place on a single day, 1 April. (This was also the day on which the novel was published – not that the apposite timing did sales any good.) Fittingly, given this propitious date, it is a novel about fools and fooling – the 'Confidence-Man' of the title is just that, a con man. Detailing a voyage along the Mississippi river, Melville's novel takes the form of a series of stories told by the passengers on board the steamboat, one of whom is the confidence trickster – then a new idiom in American society – trying to get one over on his fellow travellers. One of the passengers was probably based on Edgar Allan Poe, no stranger to hoaxes and con tricks himself. (One of Poe's short stories, 'The Balloon-Hoax', had detailed an entirely fictional trip across the Atlantic in a gas balloon, but presented the event as genuine; a credulous public was well and truly gulled, and the newspaper that had published Poe's story had to issue a retraction.) *The Confidence-Man* was a book to make readers think, its style playfully ambiguous and its effects subtle and gradual. Like *Moby-Dick* before it, this was not the sort of thing that people in 1850s America wanted. They wanted *Uncle Tom's Cabin*, or else something in the vein of Melville's earlier fiction.

So very few people took any notice of *The Confidence-Man*. Reviewers didn't know quite how to respond to the novel, but were unanimous in not much caring for it. One questioned whether it was even a novel at all, unwittingly anticipating the twentieth-century debates that would surround the novels of fellow one-day-action writers James Joyce and Virginia Woolf. Shortly after the book appeared, Melville's publisher went bust. Broken – and, because of the poor sales of his work, broke – Melville gave up writing novels and took a job as a customs house official. In 1982, *The Confidence-Man* was turned into an opera (of all things) by the American composer George Rochberg. It, too, was a flop. Nobody had much confidence in *The Confidence-Man*. Yet it is much admired by the small number of devotees who read it. Jack Kerouac, a hundred years later, was a fan of the novel: he opined that it was a great book to read while stoned.

## ✦ Uncle Tom ✦

The story of when Harriet met Abe has often been told. Around Thanksgiving Day 1862, American President Abraham Lincoln came face to face with Harriet Beecher Stowe, the author of the popular anti-slavery novel *Uncle Tom's Cabin*, which had been published a decade earlier, in 1852. Lincoln greeted Stowe with the words, 'So you're the little woman who wrote the book that made this great war!'

This momentous exchange – between the president who was fighting the war and the writer who'd caused it – is, like many great anecdotes, entirely apocryphal. Lincoln and Stowe may have met at the White House late in 1862, but the quotation attributed to Lincoln didn't appear in print until thirty-four years later, when Stowe's biographer, Annie Fields, published a piece in the *Atlantic Monthly* in 1896. As Daniel R. Vollaro points out in the *Journal of the Abraham Lincoln Association*, the anecdote was never verified by Stowe herself. Few biographers of Lincoln mention it, and the detailed account of the president's daily activities, *Lincoln Day by Day*, doesn't mention a meeting with Stowe. Those writers who do cite his 'little woman' line can't agree on the wording. Even Stowe's own relatives give wildly different accounts of the meeting: some say it occurred on 25 November, others on 2 December. As Arthur Riss notes in his chapter on Stowe in *The Cambridge Companion to American Novelists*, there is also the historical issue: when Stowe and Lincoln met – assuming a meeting took place – the Emancipation Proclamation had not yet been signed and nobody could be certain that the American Civil War *was* a 'war on slavery', as implied in Lincoln's (supposed) remark. Indeed, Stowe's reason for meeting with the President was to urge him to issue the Proclamation, which he duly did.

Yet Lincoln's line – apocryphal though it may be – epitomizes the influence that Stowe's novel had on the American public. After the Bible, it was the biggest-selling book of the entire nineteenth century, and it certainly played its part in raising the profile of the abolitionist cause. *Putnam's Magazine* went so far as to call it 'the first real success in book-making'. But its influence wasn't altogether positive: its portrayal of the deferential Uncle Tom perpetuated an African-American stereotype. Tom, of course, is the African slave who is quite literally 'sold down the river' – the Mississippi, in this case – by his kindly owners, in order to raise money. He ends up being bought by a brutal plantation owner, Legree, who tries to break Tom's strong Christian faith (and, indeed, almost succeeds). In the end, Legree realizes he cannot crush Tom's spirit but he can have him physically beaten. Tom ends up dying of his wounds, using his last breath to forgive Legree. The novel carries a strong message of Christian piety, embodied by the title character, but also tugged at the heartstrings of an American public that was becoming increasingly uneasy with slavery. Even if *Uncle Tom's Cabin* didn't cause the Civil War (and Lincoln never even suggested that it had), it nevertheless helped to win people over to the abolitionist cause.

The novel was published in Britain by Samuel Beeton, the husband of Mrs Beeton, who would later write the *Book of Household Management*. The book would be successful on both sides of the Atlantic, and would even spawn a subgenre of its own: 'anti-Tom' literature that challenged the representation of the slave-owning South that Stowe had put forward. The most popular of these was a novel by Mary Henderson Eastman, pointedly titled *Aunt Phillis's Cabin* and published later in the same year as Stowe's book.

# ✧ Twain's Memoirs ✧

Even if Lincoln didn't actually say the line about a book inspiring the American Civil War, it has become part of the mythology surrounding the war. Mark Twain was a neighbour of Stowe's and owned an inscribed copy of *Uncle Tom's Cabin*. Curiously, in his book *Life on the Mississippi* (1883) Twain did put forward the thesis that a novel had caused the American Civil War. But he had in mind another, more surprising, work: Sir Walter Scott's *Ivanhoe*, published over forty years before the outbreak of the war.

According to Twain, whereas Cervantes' *Don Quixote* had disabused the world of the romantic notion of chivalry, *Ivanhoe* had restored it. Its rosy notion of medieval feudalism particularly caught on in the South during the mid-nineteenth century, and this directly fed into the attitudes that led to the Civil War in the 1860s.

*Life on the Mississippi* is part memoir, part travel book. It contrasts antebellum (pre-Civil War) America, when a young Twain (then still Samuel Clemens) worked as a steamboat pilot on the Mississippi river, with post-war and post-slavery America in the two decades since the end of the Civil War. Twain opens with a bold claim: 'The Mississippi is well worth reading about. It is not a commonplace river, but on the contrary is in all ways remarkable. Considering the Missouri its main branch, it is the longest river in the world – four thousand three hundred miles.' (This does make it the longest river in the world, narrowly beating the Nile into second place; unfortunately for Twain, nobody else counts the Missouri as a branch of the Mississippi.) The rest of the book makes good on this opening statement, highlighting the history of the river and the ways in which it had changed in recent years (the relatively new upstart in the world of transport, the railroad, had given the river a run for its money). At its core it is an elegy for a vanished way of life.

Twain and the Mississippi were curiously intertwined from very early on in the writer's life. He owed his pen name to it: it was while he worked as a young pilot on the steamboats that he first heard the cry 'By the mark twain!', the leadsmen's traditional call signalling that the river was two fathoms deep at that point. The young Samuel Clemens remembered the term when he later launched his career as a writer.

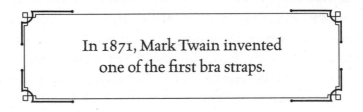

In 1871, Mark Twain invented one of the first bra straps.

*Life on the Mississippi* has a curious claim to fame, which is that it was the first book – at least the first one by a high-profile author – to have been 'written' on a typewriter. Many people think the book in question was Twain's 1876 novel *The Adventures of Tom Sawyer*, partly because Twain himself repeated the myth in his *Autobiography*; it seems, on the contrary, that *Life on the Mississippi* should instead have that honour. Twain himself didn't prepare the typescript for the book, since the typewriter he purchased in 1874 made him so angry it generated a string of expletives (as Twain himself said, 'When angry, count to four; when very angry, swear') and he was compelled to give the machine away. So he dictated *Life on the Mississippi* instead. Curiously, the recent history lurking behind Twain's book was also linked to the development of the modern typewriter: Remington, the company that produced Twain's own machine, had manufactured many of the rifles used during the Civil War.

## ✧ The Quintessential Girls' Story ✧

Although Ernest Hemingway famously remarked that all American literature comes from 'one book by Mark Twain called *Huckleberry Finn*', not everyone was a fan. Louisa May Alcott, for one. Along with her fellow New England friends (who included such influential luminaries as Henry David Thoreau and Ralph Waldo Emerson), she went so far as to try to get the book banned. 'If Mr. Clemens cannot think of something better to tell our pure-minded lads and lasses, he had best stop writing for them.' What is so remarkable about all this is that Alcott was a progressive in many respects, believing in racial equality and rights for women. She was the first woman to register to vote in Concord, Massachusetts (in school committee elections). What's more, for many years Alcott didn't want to write for the pure-minded 'lasses' either. Yet when she did so, in 1868, she produced one of the great classics of what is now known as 'young adult' fiction: *Little Women*.

On the face of it, few writers seemed less likely to produce the quintessential girls' story than Louisa May Alcott. Before writing *Little Women*, she wrote thrillers, 'lurid' romances and adventure stories under pen names such as A. M. Barnard, Oranthy

Bluggage and Minerva Moody, with titles like *Pauline's Passion and Punishment* and *The Mysterious Key and What It Opened*. The girls' story was not her literary genre of choice. In fact, she admitted in her journal that she'd never liked girls. (Whether she included her younger self in this estimation is not clear.) She didn't even want to write *Little Women*, but her publisher was keen on the idea. She herself considered such books 'moral pap for the young'. If so, they were, as her publishers realized, nevertheless potentially lucrative pap. She agreed to give it a go, though she found the story 'dull' while she was writing it. Her working title was 'The Pathetic Family'; it was her publisher, Niles, who suggested she name it *Little Women*. It's a canny title, eschewing the associations with *girls'* stories and instead suggesting adolescence, with all its trials, traumas and responsibilities (at least, those fit for print in the nineteenth century). She based the characters on her own sisters; Jo was a self-portrait.

*Little Women* became a phenomenon. In his *Sketches from Concord* (1895), Frank Preston Stearns recalled: 'Grave merchants and lawyers on their way down town in the morning said to each other: "Have you read *Little Women*?" and laughed as they said it.' (The old ones, after all, are the best.) The novel also marked a sea change in the nature of the girls' story. They had always been popular: before Alcott's novel the most successful had been *The Wide, Wide World* by 'Elizabeth Wetherell' (really Susan B. Warner), published in 1850, which rivalled even *Uncle Tom's Cabin* in its status as a bestseller. But girls' stories tended to be overly moralistic in their tone and marred by effusive sentimentality. Alcott's novel changed all that, instead depicting ordinary girls' lives in a way that real little women could relate to. Many of the incidents that feature in *Little Women* were, revealingly, based on events that the Alcott girls had actually experienced.

Alcott lived long enough to see Mark Twain's *Huckleberry Finn* published in 1885 (and to fail to have it banned). She died in 1888, just two days after her father. Curiously, father and daughter also shared a birthday.

## ⬦ Poetry – Dashed Off ⬦

Massachusetts has brought America its fair share of female writers, ever since Anne Bradstreet arrived there in 1630. Louisa May Alcott emerged as the most prominent female writer to hail from Massachusetts, becoming a literary celebrity thanks to *Little Women* and its sequels. But while Alcott was reaping the royalties from her bestselling novels, a fellow Massachusetts resident was writing in obscurity.

Her name was Emily Dickinson (1830–86), and fewer than a dozen of her many poems – she wrote some 1,800 – would be published during her lifetime. (Several appeared in an 1864 anthology, *Drum Beat*, published to raise money for Union soldiers fighting in the Civil War.) It was four years after her death, in 1890, that a book of her poetry would appear before the American public for the first time.

Like her fellow nineteenth-century American poet Walt Whitman, Dickinson refused to play by the accepted rules of poetic composition. Whitman was a pioneer of free verse – unrhymed poetry – which Robert Frost sniffily referred to as 'playing tennis with the net down'. If that analogy holds true, Dickinson barely even bothered to use a racket. Many of her poems didn't rhyme. She favoured the quatrain (four-line) form beloved of balladeers, but didn't use the regular rhythm and metre normally found in such poetry, nor did her poems tend to have much in the way of traditional narrative. She didn't bother to give most of her poems titles. She insisted on peppering her lines with dashes, which would become her trademark but which baffled initial readers and publishers, many of whom quietly altered the poetry to make it more acceptable to nineteenth-century conservative tastes. Hers was another declaration of literary independence, but recognition of such innovative style would only come posthumously.

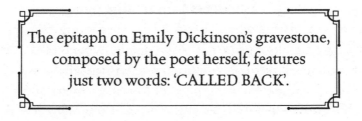

The epitaph on Emily Dickinson's gravestone, composed by the poet herself, features just two words: 'CALLED BACK'.

The things she chose to write about, too, were often odd, eccentric – in a word, 'unpoetic'. Many poets had tackled the topic of death before, but it was Dickinson who focused on the fly buzzing around the deathbed where the poem's speaker takes her final breaths. Hope is not a singing bird in Dickinson's poetry, as it is in, say, the poetry of her contemporary from across the Atlantic, Christina Rossetti: instead, hope is, more elliptically, a 'thing with feathers'. Time and again in her poems, Dickinson does what many of the truly great poets do, and wrests language into new shapes, describing falling snow as 'alabaster wool' which places a 'crystal veil' over everything, transforming familiar objects into ghosts. Indeed, the poem I just quoted from doesn't even mention that it is describing snow. It doesn't have to.

Some of her nearest and dearest knew she wrote poetry, but it wasn't until after her death that they realized just how many poems Dickinson had written. Around eight hundred of them were collected into little manuscript books which Dickinson herself lovingly put together without telling anyone. As the scholar Judith Farr has noted, Emily Dickinson was far better known as a gardener than as a poet in her own lifetime.

## ✧ Looking Forward ✧

The garden city movement is not, perhaps, one of the best-known socio-political movements in American history, but it set the scene for a number of modern towns and cities in both the United States and Britain. Essentially, it was an early twentieth-century initiative designed to make cities nicer, cleaner, and above all, *greener* places to live, and gave rise to a different form of town planning, spearheaded by an Englishman named Ebenezer Howard.

It's a little-known fact that Howard's idea for the garden city was largely inspired by one of the bestselling American novels of the late nineteenth century. Edward Bellamy's 1888 novel *Looking Backward: 2000–1887* tells of a young American, Julian West, who, like Rip Van Winkle before him in the annals of American literature, falls asleep only to wake up to find himself over a century into the future, in the year 2000. Bellamy's imagined future is, in some ways, uncannily close to the millennial reality that came to pass: it's a world of credit cards, radio stations and electronic broadcasting, among other modern inventions. And in other respects, Bellamy didn't so much predict the future as help to make it, given his novel's role in inspiring the garden city movement.

In other respects, his book somewhat missed the mark, forecasting a world in which people only had to work for a few hours a day (if only), could retire in their forties (as if), and poverty had been eradicated. Bellamy disliked the word 'socialism', preferring to talk of Nationalism, but there's no doubt that his is a socialist utopia. Indeed, Bellamy's book is in the utopian tradition named by Sir Thomas More in the sixteenth century, and was conceived, according to its author, as 'a cloud palace for an ideal humanity'. Seeing the 'horrid world' that America had become since the Civil War, with corrupt government officials and a vast gulf between the richest and the poorest of the country, Bellamy set about imagining a sublime Arcadia, one fit for his children and his children's children to live in. His book was more than a novel: it was a blueprint for a new society, part socialist manifesto and part science fiction. American readers couldn't get enough of it. Within two years of the novel's publication, 162 'Bellamy Clubs' had been founded in the USA. After *Ben-Hur* and *Uncle Tom's Cabin*, it's estimated that *Looking Backward* was the biggest-selling American novel published in the entire nineteenth century.

This success was largely down to the fact that many Americans shared Bellamy's grim view of the America in which they lived: plagued by a series of economic recessions, ravaged by industrialism, racked by political scandal. They, too, longed for a better world – specifically, a better *America* – and *Looking*

*Backward* helped them to look forward to something brighter that was, his novel suggested, just around the bend. Unfortunately, the world the novel tried to will into existence never came – but he did help others to imagine, and attempt to create, a better kind of urban space, where houses and factories were built side by side with parks and trees, making cities healthier and more aesthetically pleasant places to live and work. And he got the bit about credit cards right.

# ✥ Out of the Wild West ✥

Most people know the Charlton Heston film *Ben-Hur*, but the novel – itself a bestseller in its day – doesn't loom quite so large in the popular consciousness. It's reckoned by at least one estimate that Lew Wallace's 1880 novel even outsold that other runaway bestseller of nineteenth-century American fiction, *Uncle Tom's Cabin*. In the first seven months it shifted 3,000 copies, but it would go on to be a runaway hit.

The novel's protagonist, Judah Ben-Hur – a figure invented by Wallace, and unknown in historical accounts – is a Jewish nobleman and prince who is taken as a slave by the Romans (fitted up on a false charge of attempted murder, when a piece of his roof accidentally dropped on the Roman parade passing his house). Eventually, he becomes a charioteer in the Roman games. The novel cleverly parallels Ben-Hur's story with that of Jesus (its subtitle is *A Tale of the Christ*), another Jewish figure living under Roman occupation in the same part of the world, and at the same time. No doubt this Christian subplot helped it to become the blockbuster hit of its day. It was even beatified by the Pope, Leo XIII – the first work of fiction to be so honoured.

Indeed, *Ben-Hur* is often seen as the greatest Christian novel of the entire nineteenth century, which is odd given that the book's author was self-confessedly ignorant of Christianity, was not a Christian and never belonged to any of its many sects. Wallace later attributed the germ of the book to a conversation he had on a train with Colonel Robert Ingersoll in 1876, during which the two men discussed Christianity and Wallace concluded that he didn't know enough about the religion. He resolved to look into it more, with a view to writing about the history of Christianity and the life of Jesus Christ. But his efforts to improve his own religious knowledge led to the idea of writing his celebrated novel of chariot-racing, friendship, betrayal, revenge, Christianity, and the importance of having a good tiler to do your roof.

> The screenplay for the 1959 MGM film was the work of many hands, including Gore Vidal and Christopher Fry (best remembered for his historical verse drama *The Lady's Not for Burning*).

*Ben-Hur* had already been filmed for the big screen twice before the blockbuster 1959 epic starring Charlton Heston in the title role. Both of the previous film adaptations were silent movies, made in 1907 and 1925. There are rumours that some of the extras involved in the pivotal chariot-racing scene died during the making of the 1959 version, but this is untrue – though one unfortunate stuntman did die during the filming of the chariot-race scene for the 1925 movie. The 1959 film swept the board at the Oscars that year, winning an unprecedented eleven Academy Awards, a record that would not be equalled until 1997, when *Titanic* picked up eleven gongs.

*Ben-Hur* was Wallace's most successful novel, and none of his other books came close to matching its success. (Wallace himself thought his best novel was *The Prince of India; or, Why Constantinople Fell*; the rest of the world disagreed.) But *Ben-Hur* is not the only piece of his writing that has been of lasting interest, because Wallace also corresponded with Billy the Kid. Wild West aficionados have pored over the author's letters to the notorious outlaw ever since. In 1879, the year before he published *Ben-Hur*, Wallace – who had been made governor of New Mexico in 1878 – struck a deal with Billy the Kid, promising to get him immunity from prosecution if Henry McCarty (the Kid's real name) agreed to testify against some other criminals. After considering the offer, the Kid agreed – though the district attorney dismissed Wallace's order and detained McCarty anyway. Billy the Kid would later escape from the jail, surviving on the run for two years until he was shot dead by sheriff Pat Garrett.

# ON THE CONTINENT

While everything the last few chapters have explored – Enlightenment, revolution, Romanticism, the forging of a national identity – was occurring in Britain and America, things were afoot on the Continent. What was different about Europe? In some ways, very little: countries such as France and Germany produced their own Enlightenment figures, their own Romantic poets, and a fair number of 'national' figures – Goethe for Germany, Tolstoy for Russia, Victor Hugo (among many others) for France.

But in other respects there was something distinctive about European literature. For one – as the first couple of entries below demonstrate – that perennial literary genre the fairy tale came of age on the Continent, being transferred from an oral tradition to the pages of a book with great ease and, it must be said, staggering popularity. For another, numerous European novelists, especially Russians like Tolstoy and Dostoevsky, seemed to be one step ahead of their anglophone contemporaries in lifting the lid on the human mind and examining all of the distasteful or nasty bits that lurked within. At the end of the nineteenth century, this spirit of psychological enquiry would be appearing not only in the pages of novels but within influential scholarly studies, such as the early works of Sigmund Freud, father of psychoanalysis. (Freud himself, I might add, was interested in fairy tales and folklore, especially for what they revealed about mankind's primal fears and drives.)

This chapter, then, goes on to the Continent but also into the deepest and darkest parts of the human soul. It promises to be quite the library tour.

## ✦ Madame's Fairy Tales ✦

The year 1697 saw the publication in France of two new collections of fairy tales. One of these, by Charles Perrault, would later be translated into English under the title *Tales of Mother Goose*. The book introduced English readers to many classic characters for the first time: Cinderella, Sleeping Beauty, Puss in Boots, Bluebeard and Little Red Riding Hood all became known in England thanks to Perrault. The other volume of fairy tales published that year was written by the relatively unknown Marie-Catherine Le Jumel de Barneville, Baroness d'Aulnoy (1650/1–1705) – better known as Madame d'Aulnoy, though barely known at all these days.

In 1690, d'Aulnoy published the first fairy tale ever to appear in France, three years before Perrault published his first. Then, in 1697, she published a collection of stories under the title *Les contes des fées* – 'fairy tales'. It's the origin of the term that has been used to describe such stories ever since.

D'Aulnoy's heroines in her fairy tales are often unconventional, plucky and resourceful, and in this respect they are obvious mirrors of their author. Forced into an arranged marriage as a teenager with a man thirty years her senior – who also happened to be a dissolute gambler – she would later separate from her husband and have a number of children by various lovers – behaviour that got her ostracized from the aristocratic circles in which she moved. Her fairy tales were written in order to win her way back into the social clique that had rejected her. Despite her growing brood of mouths to feed, she didn't write with her own or anyone else's children in mind, instead addressing her stories to the adults she knew in Paris literary salons. It evidently worked: she was known in France as '*la reine de la féerie*', 'queen of the fairies'. Abroad, too, readers couldn't get enough of her: in the eighteenth century it is reckoned there were as many as twenty-two editions of her fairy tales published, though the actual number may have been even higher.

D'Aulnoy's importance in the history of the fairy tale is partly to do with her gender: in her stories she is more interested than her male contemporaries in what it is like to be a woman, whether parlour maid, princess or queen, in such a world. A number of her tales are variations on the 'beauty and the beast' motif, though d'Aulnoy was writing before the story of *Beauty and the Beast* was written. Indeed, her own fairy tales almost certainly influenced the female author of that story, Gabrielle-Suzanne Barbot de Villeneuve.

Equally curious is her role in the development of the Goldilocks character in children's literature. 'Goldilocks' first appears in print in English in the mid-sixteenth century, used simply to describe someone with golden hair. The famous story involving the three bears was first written down by Robert Southey, one of the Lake Poets and one of Britain's longest-serving Poets Laureate, who published it in 1837. Southey's version doesn't refer to the female character as Goldilocks and the three bears are all bachelors rather than the family unit they later evolved into. Conversely, d'Aulnoy's 'The Story of Pretty Goldilocks' is strong on the Goldilocks element but distinctly lacking in bears. It appears that the two stories merged early in the twentieth century, giving us the tale we now know.

Why isn't d'Aulnoy as famous as Perrault or, later, Hans Christian Andersen and the Brothers Grimm in the annals of fairy tales? Why don't titles like 'The Little Good Mouse', 'The Imp Prince' or 'The Yellow Dwarf' leap to mind as 'Sleeping Beauty' or 'Puss in Boots' do? For starters, her stories do not contain the same widespread appeal across all levels of society. Rather than use the 'rags to riches' narrative that is so beloved of fairy-tale writers, d'Aulnoy writes about high-born characters whose nosedive into the squalid world of the 'common' people is temporary, their rightful status being restored by the end of the story. This is even true of d'Aulnoy's take on the Cinderella tale, 'Finette Cendron'. When the French Revolution disturbed the entire social fabric of France a hundred years later, it would be Perrault's orphan Cinderella and her glass slipper, rather than d'Aulnoy's Finette Cendron with her red velvet shoe, who would be fixed in readers' memories.

The other reason she has not lasted into the twenty-first century can be summed up in two words: Walt Disney. When Disney wanted a classic fairy tale to translate to the big screen, it was to Perrault, Andersen and the Brothers Grimm that he turned, rather than d'Aulnoy.

But despite her later neglect, d'Aulnoy did retain her popularity in England well into the nineteenth century, and during the Victorian era she was paid the compliment that all great writers of fairy tales are paid: her work was turned into popular pantomimes.

## ✧ Little Hans ✧

Like the sad clown, the idea of the unhappy children's author has become a cliché. Writers who bring so much joy to others – especially at that crucial time in our lives when the world seems full of magic and possibility – have tended to be plagued by depression, loneliness and melancholy. Lewis Carroll, Edward Lear and Beatrix Potter are just three examples. But perhaps, of all the great writers for children, none has exemplified this familiar trope more clearly than Hans Christian Andersen, Denmark's finest literary export.

> When staying in hotels, Hans Christian Andersen always carried a coil of rope with him in case he needed to escape from a fire.

Part of the problem was that, from a very young age, Andersen was not easy to get along with: conceited beyond belief, self-absorbed to the point of egotism, and determined to shut himself away from others in order to pursue his literary calling. He admired, and met, a number of the leading literary men of the day (and they were almost invariably men), including Victor Hugo and, disastrously, Charles Dickens. Andersen went to stay with Dickens and his family in 1857, but outstayed his welcome somewhat – by about three weeks. Dickens's daughters found the fairy-tale writer a terrible bore, and everyone's patience eventually wore very thin. When Andersen finally left, Dickens unleashed his long-contained frustration on the mirror in the guest room, writing: 'Hans Andersen slept in this room for five weeks — which seemed to the family AGES!' That was the end of the friendship between the two writers.

It's tempting to see the stories that Andersen wrote – the first volume of which, *Fairy Tales*, was published in 1835 – as a reflection of his life. It's true that many feature a lone outsider of some kind: 'The Ugly Duckling', perhaps most famously, though 'The Little Mermaid' is another example, as is the boy whose honest cry at the end of 'The Emperor's New Clothes' cuts across the lies and sycophancy of the townspeople. Perhaps of all the fairy-tale writers, Andersen writes best about the loner, the social outcast, the one who doesn't fit in.

Andersen also harboured disastrous infatuations with a number of women, among them the celebrated Swedish operatic soprano Jenny Lind, and he clearly felt sexual desire as much as the next person. He would mark in his diary every time he masturbated, which he apparently did rather a lot. It's now believed that he was bisexual, though he remained a lifelong bachelor and, those marks in his diary aside, a celibate. When he died, a long letter from a woman named Riborg Voigt, for whom Andersen had harboured an unrequited affection in his youth, was found lying on his chest.

The famous statue in Copenhagen of one of Andersen's best-loved creations, the Little Mermaid, was commissioned in 1909 by Carl Jacobsen, the man after whom Carlsberg beer was named. Fittingly, Andersen was a fan of Danish beers: another brewery, Albani, have even named one of their ales after him.

## ✧ True Confessions ✧

The Swiss Enlightenment figure Jean-Jacques Rousseau (1712–78) is remembered for a number of achievements. His 1762 work *The Social Contract* is deemed an important contribution to political philosophy and later helped to stoke the fires of the French Revolution. But it is his 1781 book *Confessions* that represents his most important legacy. Indeed, pretty much anyone who has written their autobiography since has owed Rousseau some sort of debt, for he was the one who did more than anyone else to create the modern notion of autobiography. Rousseau's *Confessions* effectively invented the genre.

Before the *Confessions*, not many public figures were prepared to spill the beans about the intimate details of their private lives: their regrets, their desires, their most unsavoury secrets. But Rousseau bared all, or virtually all, in his *Confessions*. The book's title calls to mind St Augustine's *Confessions*, written over thirteen centuries earlier and often viewed as the first work of autobiography. But whereas Augustine's focus is on the spiritual life – as was still the case a thousand years later when

Margery Kempe dictated tales of her life of religious devotion in the fifteenth century – Rousseau's memoirs are firmly rooted in the temporal, physical world. His is the first secular work of autobiography to have a significant influence.

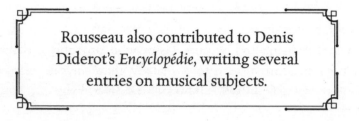

Rousseau also contributed to Denis Diderot's *Encyclopédie*, writing several entries on musical subjects.

In the *Confessions*, Rousseau chronicles everything from his masturbation (which he describes as a 'dangerous supplement') to his regret at having put all five of his children in an orphanage. He was, in some respects, a hypocrite, calling for operas and plays to be banned, yet happy to write both himself. In later life he became increasingly paranoid, convinced that his friends were out to defame him. Rousseau may be one of the greatest memoirists the world has seen, but as a human being he had more than his fair share of flaws. Indeed, it was his social and moral deficiencies that helped him to become a great memoirist. He is not afraid to examine his own desires and obsessions, or to air his keenest regrets.

As a consequence we, the readers, feel as if we are being personally confided in. No wonder Rousseau is sometimes viewed as an early Romantic figure: his writing exhibits an interest in the self and in the primacy of personal experience which we will later find enthusiastically endorsed in the poetry of Wordsworth, Keats, and a host of other figures. Rousseau's self-absorption and egotism also enabled him to write a pioneering work of self-examination. Autobiographies have effectively been a long list of their author's 'confessions' ever since.

## ✧ The Dangers of Reading ✧

It was a man named Samuel Tissot who probably did more to turn masturbation into a malady than anyone else: his 1760 essay *L'Onanisme* drew on his knowledge of young masturbators whom he'd observed first-hand (as it were), and argued that the loss of seminal fluid from the body led to gout, headaches, blurred vision, rheumatism and much else besides. Tissot's books were taken up and read by a great number of people – his general study of health, the 1761 book *Avis au peuple sur sa santé*, is reckoned to have been the medical bestseller of the century – and the Victorians inherited Tissot's view that 'self-abuse' or 'self-pollution' (as it was often known) had a debilitating effect on young men's health and virility.

It's easy to laugh at Tissot – indeed, it's pretty much compulsory – but elsewhere he did make valuable contributions to medical science. His study of migraines is now seen as one of the first great scientific pieces on the subject, and he was an important writer on epilepsy, then still a much-misunderstood condition.

And Tissot also wrote an intriguing little book specifically tackling those illnesses suffered by students and learned men: *An Essay on Diseases Incidental to Literary and Sedentary Persons, With proper rule for preventing their fatal consequences and instructions for their cure*, published in 1766. Its essential thesis is that while study is beneficial to the mind, it can be damaging to the body.

Tissot's specific focus was on those gentlemen who had the money and leisure to pursue study at great length, and who were therefore at the greatest risk of succumbing to various diseases. Alexander Pope was half-right: a *lot* of learning certainly did appear to be a dangerous thing. Tissot cites the case of 'a public promotion' at which 'one of the candidates for literary honour after having pursued his studies with the most arduous application both day and night, through a too great attention to his oration, that he might be able to say it accurately by heart, was suddenly seized with a catalepsy and fell down'. He also tells of a mathematician who 'hastened a paroxysm by applying a long time to the solution of a difficult problem'. A Frenchman made all his hair fall out by studying too hard for four months: 'his beard fell first, then his eye-lashes, then his eye-brows, then the hair of his head, and finally all the hair of his body.'

Studying, Tissot argued throughout his book, could be a dangerous pastime. Presumably his own book on the dangers of reading came with a health warning. But in a way he was right: we may think that our concern over sitting down at our desks all day is a modern phenomenon, the product of our middle-class, white-collar jobs, but Tissot was addressing it some 250 years ago.

## ✧ The Glums ✧

While he was writing – or trying to write – *Les Misérables*, Victor Hugo found himself suffering from colygraphia – better known as 'writer's block'. So he decided to shed all his clothes, take himself off to a room where he had only pen and paper for company, and force himself to sit down and write, without even the distraction of clothes to derail him from his task. His servants reportedly had orders that they weren't to return them until he had written something. He worked on *Les Misérables* for many years, beginning work on it in the 1840s but not finishing it until 1862. He must've given his clothes up hundreds of times.

*Les Misérables* focuses on the convict Jean Valjean, who is imprisoned for stealing bread to feed his family. He later reforms his ways and rises up the social ranks, though his criminal past will come back to haunt him. It's a vast narrative about crime and punishment, sin and redemption, love and family, poverty and wealth, and much else besides. The novel was reportedly the most popular novel among soldiers in the American Civil War. Published in 1862, the book had begun to appear in the USA in an English translation before that year was out, and Hugo's epic tale struck a chord with both Unionists and Confederates.

Much like Herman Melville's *Moby-Dick*, published a decade earlier (though as we've seen, not a novel that Americans, military or otherwise, exactly rushed to read), Hugo's vast novel contains considerable sections which don't move the plot forward but which shed light on nineteenth-century Paris and act as signposts for the novel's major themes. Like Dickens, Hugo is a master storyteller, but one who isn't afraid to build lengthy asides (essentially, whole essays) into a novel in order to remind the reader of their social duty in fighting poverty and seeking to make the world in which they live a happier place. Hugo digresses so that he can discuss everything from organized religion to the building of the city's sewers. One colossal section of the novel describes with painstaking detail the battle of Waterloo, which makes for great reading but has absolutely nothing to do with the plot. Only in the final brief chapter of this nineteen-chapter extravaganza does Hugo bring things back to the main narrative of his book.

Despite the book's popularity, it was something of a critical flop upon its publication in America. Now widely regarded as Hugo's masterpiece, it met with mostly negative reviews. The *New Englander* had this to say: 'The whole career of Jean Valjean presents a series of impossible cases, of strange incongruities, and stands in continuous antagonism with the principles of truth and honor which ought to be every honest man's line of conduct.' Even the *New York Times*, which praised the novel as 'remarkable' and 'brilliant', also went on to call Hugo 'a prosy madman' – something of a mixed review, after all.

## ⟡ Verne's Uncanny Prediction ⟡

Jean Jules Verne, great-grandson of the famous French author, was obsessed as a young boy by an old bronze safe that had been handed down from one family generation to the next. The safe was locked, and most family members believed it to be nothing but an empty old chest. Why, then, should it have been locked? The young Verne knew the safe had once belonged to his famous great-grandfather, and the boy harboured dreams of the treasures that might be lying within. Unfortunately, the lock was well and truly secure, and the contents of the safe thus remained a mystery for decades.

Then, one day in 1989, his curiosity got the better of him. Verne called for a locksmith and the safe was opened, its contents revealed at last. Inside there was a little yellow notebook containing the manuscript of a novel written by his great-grandfather over a century before, but never published. The novel had been written in 1863 but set in the then far-off future world of 1960. It described a world in which people drive motorcars powered by internal combustion and travel to work in driverless trains. Their houses are lit by electric light. They use fax machines, telephones and computers, and live in skyscrapers furnished with elevators and television. Their criminals are executed using the electric chair. Greek and Latin are no longer widely taught in schools, and the French language has been 'corrupted' by borrowings from the English. People shop in huge department stores, and the streets are adorned with advertisements in electric lights. Money has become everyone's god. The novel also describes a tall structure in Paris, an electric lighthouse that can be seen for miles around. This was in 1863; the Eiffel Tower would not be built until 1889.

*Paris in the Twentieth Century* could have been published in 1863, but instead it languished away until it was discovered over eighty years after its author's death. The novel was eventually published in 1994, with an English translation following two years later.

> Jules Verne is the most translated French author ever, and the second-most translated author in the world, after Agatha Christie and ahead of Shakespeare.

Why did it take over 130 years for the novel to see the light of day? When he completed *Paris in the Twentieth Century* in 1863, Verne had already published a successful novel, *Five Weeks in a Balloon*, but his publisher was reluctant to publish his next offering because he thought the story was too unbelievable and feared readers wouldn't take it seriously. 'No one today will believe your prophecy,' he told the dejected author. Ironically, it is probably the most prophetic of all Verne's books. Verne abandoned his plans to publish the novel, locked it away and turned to other projects. He was at the start of a promising career as a novelist: Victor Hugo had been an early influence, particularly Hugo's plays, but the young author had now started to find his way as a writer of a new kind of fiction. *Paris in the Twentieth Century* is full of the kinds of inventive ideas often found in the work of a young writer just embarking on his career.

The unwitting hero of Verne's novel is Michel Dufrenoy, a teenage poet who finds himself homeless in an uncaring city governed by money, technology, and above all, paperwork. In an eerie foreshadowing of the modern world, bureaucracy is everywhere. It's an uncannily prescient novel. It's a shame that the story is so flat – so much so that it is almost non-existent – since the world Verne creates is vividly realized, bleakly pessimistic, and (perhaps these qualities are not mutually exclusive) extraordinarily like our own. But then dystopian fiction – a genre that was embraced more by the century in which Verne's novel is set than the one in which it was written – often privileges detailed world-building over the demands of a page-turning plot.

Verne might easily have thrown in the towel following the rejection of his early novel, but instead he persevered – producing, over the next decade, all of his most famous and enduring novels: *Journey to the Centre of the Earth, From the Earth to the Moon* and its sequel *Around the Moon, Twenty Thousand Leagues under the Sea*, and, perhaps most famous, *Around the World in Eighty Days*. All of these books are still in print. But *Paris in the Twentieth Century* would have to wait another century to see the light of day. The year in which it is set, 1960, had already been and gone by the time the novel was available to buy in bookshops.

# ✦ All's Well That Ends Well ✦

Lev Tolstoy, to give him his Russian name ('Leo' is only the English version), is known as a great novelist, but he was also a gifted illustrator, who drew scenes from Jules Verne's *Twenty Thousand Leagues under the Sea* for his children. But of course it's not for his drawings that he's remembered. *Anna Karenina* is one of the greatest tragic novels of the nineteenth century. Even more famous than that, though, is *War and Peace*.

*War and Peace* is one of those great unread novels that many people know about but few have read all the way through. How much of what we think we know about it is, after all, accurate? It's commonly thought to be the longest novel ever written – well, the longest world-famous one anyway – but several famous novels, among them Samuel Richardson's eighteenth-century epistolary romp *Clarissa*, Victor Hugo's *Les Misérables* and Vikram Seth's *A Suitable Boy*, are longer. Proust's *A la recherche du temps perdu* is viewed as a single novel, but is told over the course of a whopping seven volumes. To make the issue even more complicated, *War and Peace* isn't even a novel in the usual sense: Tolstoy considered it more of a historical chronicle. Of course, it's fiction rather than fact, but Tolstoy grounds the lives of his invented characters in a very real, meticulously researched historical Russia. Indeed, he drops the names of many real historical personages into the novel – chiefly, of course, Napoleon Bonaparte, though there are many others.

The novel – sorry, *chronicle* – is set during Napoleon's invasion of Russia between the years 1805 and 1812, and focuses chiefly on the fortunes of five families: the Bezukhovs, the Bolkonskys, the Rostovs, the Kuragins and the Drubetskoys. One of Tolstoy's aims in writing such a vast work was to undermine the popular nineteenth-century idea of history as a series of actions carried out by 'great men' – men such as Napoleon, for instance. History has always been more complex than that, with a whole range of factors affecting its course, as well as the everyday lives of ordinary people. How much of our lives is in our control, and how many things that happen to us are a result of outside factors?

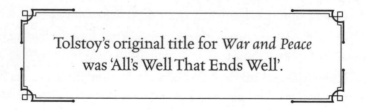

Tolstoy's original title for *War and Peace* was 'All's Well That Ends Well'.

Tolstoy was dissatisfied with the ending of the book, even after it had been published. He later disowned all of his earlier novels following his conversion to a form of Christianity that also involved him giving up much of his vast wealth. He alienated his wife, Sophia, over many years, and eventually left her, a few days before his death from pneumonia, at a railway station, in 1910. But forty years earlier, when he'd written *War and Peace*, Sophia had helped him by slavishly copying out the entire manuscript for him, in longhand, seven times – which is probably as heroic an act as anything that happens in the book itself.

## ✥ Under the Floorboards ✥

We tend to think of existentialism – if we think of it at all – as a twentieth-century idea. Sartre, Camus, and all those Frenchmen wearing long coats with the collars turned up, smoking in Parisian doorways and wondering how we can go about creating personal meaning for our lives in a random and indifferent universe. But the nineteenth century laid the groundwork for these later philosophical ruminations. The work of the Danish philosopher Søren Kierkegaard (1813–55) provides an important precursor, but so does Dostoevsky's first major book, *Notes from the Underground* (1864).

*Notes from the Underground* is, in many ways, a decidedly inaccurate translation of the original Russian title, which is rendered more faithfully into English as 'Notes from under the Ground' or even 'Notes from under the Floorboards'. This short novel focuses on an unnamed retired Russian civil servant, generally referred to by critics as the 'Underground Man', who bitterly ponders where his life went wrong, subjects the big questions to his weary scrutiny, meets a prostitute, goes to bed with her, bonds with her and then alienates her in his rage. Such a potted summary hardly conveys the psychological intensity of the book, or Dostoevsky's profound understanding of what makes the Underground Man – and, to an extent, all men – tick. What drives men to seek revenge, to lash out at women, to square up to other men, and to become consumed with anger and frustration? Few writers before Dostoevsky had dared shine a light quite so intently on the dark and filthy recesses of the human mind, the unpleasant aspects of the (usually male) psyche; Dostoevsky was prepared not only to point the light there but to poke what he uncovered with a big stick. Robert Louis Stevenson once described reading *Crime and Punishment* as like having an illness; not a particularly enjoyable or pleasant experience, but one which induces a visceral and deeply felt reaction.

Indeed, Dostoevsky is renowned worldwide for the psychological depth he brings to his characters: few novelists, certainly few nineteenth-century novelists, are quite so good at getting inside people's heads. As James Wood observes in *How Fiction Works*, Dostoevsky pretty much single-handedly invented the psychological category that the German philosopher Friedrich Nietzsche called *ressentiment*: the sense of hostility we feel towards something which we seize upon as the cause of our inner frustration. (In this regard, it is not too far removed from the idea of the inferiority complex.) Often what we hate is closely related to what we love – indeed, we loathe something because, deep down, it makes us jealous or emulous. (Homophobic hate preachers who turn out to be secretly gay are a good example of this. So, Wood argues, is much modern terrorism, which often entails a closely intertwined love–hate relationship with the thing it wishes to destroy.)

Indeed, Nietzsche went so far as to call Dostoevsky 'the only psychologist from whom I have anything to learn'. We all have much to learn from him, and although *Crime and Punishment* and *The Brothers Karamazov* can teach us a great deal about Dostoevsky's psychological acuity (and about ourselves), the best place to start is with this short masterpiece. Those floorboards need to be lifted from time to time.

## ✧ Thus Spake Nietzsche ✧

On 3 January 1889, on the streets of Turin, Friedrich Nietzsche went mad and suffered a sudden breakdown. The (oft-repeated) story goes that Nietzsche witnessed a horse being whipped and ran to the animal to protect it. Shortly afterwards, he dropped to the ground. Nietzsche would never be the same again. Madness, it appears, ran in the family: Nietzsche's father, a Lutheran priest, had suffered from bouts of mental illness.

Even before this psychological breakdown, Nietzsche was far from a well man. He suffered from persistent migraines, nausea and poor eyesight, among many other afflictions. Insomnia was another, and, in his efforts to cure himself of one too many sleepless nights, the hapless philosopher became addicted to chloral hydrate, a sleeping drug. His poor health led to his having to retire from his professorship of classics at Basel in 1879 – a position to which he had been appointed when he was just twenty-four years old.

Nietzsche had been an apt pupil and university student (he studied at both Bonn and Leipzig) and produced his first book, *The Birth of Tragedy* (1872), while still in his late twenties. This work of literary and anthropological criticism sees civilized life as a balancing act between two impulses, the Dionysian and the Apollonian – in other words, between the forces of chaos/emotion and order/reason, of getting blind drunk on the one hand and doing one's tax returns on the other. These two forces are at work within us all at an unconscious level, much like the id and the superego in Freud's slightly later construction of the unconscious. This interest in the dual nature of man was explored by many writers at the time – novelists as well as philosophers and psychologists. It's there in Robert Louis Stevenson's *Strange Case of Dr Jekyll and Mr Hyde* (1886). This focus on man's duality can partly be attributed to Darwin's theory of evolution, which had brought home that although we may behave in a civilized fashion most of the time, underneath we are animals, driven by animal impulses. These competing forces of impulsive pleasure-seeker and responsible, conscience-stricken control freak are at war with each other everywhere in writing of the late nineteenth century.

Say Nietzsche's name to most people and they'll probably say, 'Wasn't he the one who influenced Hitler?' It's true that Adolf Hitler owned a bust of Nietzsche – but the German leader doesn't appear to have read much of his work. Nietzsche's sister Elizabeth, who became her brother's executor following his death in 1900, later distorted his work in order to lend credence to her own proto-Nazi leanings. As a result, a narrative has emerged leading straight from Nietzsche's pen to the crowds at Nuremberg. To be fair, Nietzsche didn't exactly help himself. His work is so layered and ironic in places that it readily lends itself to interpretations which are, many of his diehard fans assert, misinterpretations: Nietzsche himself, they respond, was no fascist or anti-Semite. This debate has been dividing critics of his work for some time now. The problem is that much of

Nietzsche's satire gets lost in translation or interpretation, and his ironic mockery, unfortunately, makes his attacks on anti-Semitism sound anti-Semitic. In one letter, he wrote of having all anti-Semites shot; presumably he didn't include himself among the list of the condemned.

This didn't much matter at the time, for he was virtually ignored during his lifetime. One of his most remarkable books is *Thus Spake Zarathustra* (1883–5), part philosophical tract, part literary experiment (Nietzsche was also a middling poet and even a composer – he was friends with Richard Wagner for a time, though they later fell out over the subject of Christianity). *Thus Spake Zarathustra* contains many of Nietzsche's central ideas: the idea that 'God is dead', the Eternal Recurrence (history, to put it crudely, repeats itself), and the Übermensch or Superman. These had been touched upon in Nietzsche's earlier work *The Gay Science*, but it is in *Zarathustra* that he develops them. Harold Bloom called the book 'unreadable'; it is perhaps Nietzsche's most representative work. Make of that what you will.

*Thus Spake Zarathustra* is the original 'trilogy in four parts': originally conceived as a three-part book, it was unfinished when Nietzsche wrote the third part, leading him to pen a fourth.

# ✧ Joking Aside ✧

Analysing jokes, as the old line has it, is like dissecting a frog: nobody is that interested in it, and the frog dies. But like the geeky few who sit through a magician's act and long to know how it's done, there are always some who would rather take a scalpel to the proverbial amphibian at any cost. *Knowing* how something works is more important than dwelling in a mystical and compelling state of uncertainty – what the poet Keats called 'Negative Capability'.

Unfortunately for those hovering over the dissecting table, nobody *does* know how jokes work. Not really. Yet some of the finest minds have attempted to explain the mechanics of a joke, and to explore why we crack jokes, why we laugh, and why certain jokes are 'better' than others. In the early years of the twentieth century, the French philosopher Henri Bergson turned his thoughts to the subject of laughter, concluding that it's a necessary social function and adding that we tend to laugh most heartily at jokes that turn people into things. Other thinkers, such as Sigmund Freud – best-known for his 1899 book *The Interpretation of Dreams* – approached the question of laughter and joking from a psychological perspective. His 1905 book *Jokes and Their Relation to the Unconscious* is a valiant attempt to 'psychoanalyse' the joke, to understand the unconscious impulses behind our desire to laugh at, and make, jokes.

For John Carey, writing in the introduction to a recent edition of Freud's book, Freud's study of jokes is even more original than his more famous book on dreams. Indeed, Freud's theory of jokes grew out of his work on dreams – he thought dreams use jokes as a sort of cloaking mechanism for veiling their true meanings.

One of the clearest links between the two is the humble pun, which Freud thought a common feature of dreams and which is obviously also the bedrock of many a joke. Both 'narratives' often involve a pivotal moment that condenses two different meanings into one word or image. In Freudian psychoanalysis, jokes are the funny flipside to dreams.

There aren't many laughs to be had in Freud's book on jokes. He does record some witty exchanges: hearing that Rousseau had written a poem called *Ode to Posterity*, Voltaire reportedly said, 'This poem will not reach its address.' But this is less a joke than a quip. And Freud ties himself up in knots at times, contradicting himself or else beginning to doubt, midpoint, whether his argument is even valid. Yet *Jokes and Their Relation to the Unconscious* is a useful supplement to Freud's more famous work on dreams, in suggesting possible answers to the questions: Why do we tell jokes? And why do we find them funny? What makes them pleasurable? Here, Freud seems to be accurate in suggesting that there usually needs to be a 'butt' of the joke: as in *Philogelos* over 1,500 years before, every good joke needs its Abderite or Sidonian.

# THE MODERN
# WORLD

Modernity is a difficult thing to define. When did it all begin? When did the world stop being old-fashioned and become 'modern'? Nobody can quite agree. Yet by the end of the nineteenth century and the beginning of the twentieth, it's clear that the world was changing in ways that would have been unimaginable a hundred years before – and the rate of change seemed to be accelerating.

Take technology: the decade between 1895 and 1905 alone saw the first radio transmission, the invention of cinema and the Wright Brothers' powered flight, while the modern motorcar was being developed and perfected during this busy period. Within a few decades there would be a cinema in every city, a radio in nearly every home, and planes and cars would be established modes of travel. How could writers respond to the bustling nature of the modern world?

This modern era – roughly from the end of the nineteenth century until our own time – is the subject of this final chapter.

In it we see the novel taking an experimental turn, the concept of the robot being born in an obscure Czech play, and numerous new efforts to categorize the modern world, from A through to Z.

## ✦ In Search of Proust ✦

It's probably the most acclaimed novel about going to bed ever written. It's very literally a 'book at bedtime', or at least, a book *of* bedtime. It's also perhaps the longest well-known novel ever written. It might additionally take the crown for 'best moment involving a cake and a cup of tea' in all of fiction.

The novel is *A la recherche du temps perdu*, at least in the original French. What to call it in English remains a tricky issue: it's been translated as both *Remembrance of Things Past* (after a phrase from a Shakespeare sonnet) and *In Search of Lost Time*. The latter is probably more favoured these days. The novel, written by Marcel Proust (1871–1922) over the course of many years and published between 1913 and 1927, spans seven whopping volumes and nearly one-and-a-half million words. No wonder the Monty Python team found it so hard to summarize.

The most famous two bits of this heptalogy, though, are to be found in the first book, *Du côté de chez Swann* (*Swann's Way* or *The Way by Swann's*, depending on which English translation you opt for), which may have something to do with how far most intrepid readers get in Proust's voluminous narrative. It's a narrative devoted, perhaps above all else, to memory and time, as the English titles for the whole novel suggest. The first famous thing about the book is the moment when Marcel, the novel's narrator, is eating a madeleine (a little cake) and drinking a cup of tea, when all of a sudden he finds his mind transported back to his childhood. (I say 'all of a sudden' but it takes him numerous pages and many long sentences to get back there.) The second famous thing about Proust's novel is the long description of going to bed that it provides: Marcel recalls how, in his childhood at the family home at Combray, his mother would put him to bed. It may not sound like a promising start for a long novel, but – as with many modernists – Proust's method is to slow down and examine in detail how our memories function and exactly *how* we experience the world around us. It's thin on action, instead favouring psychological intensity and complexity.

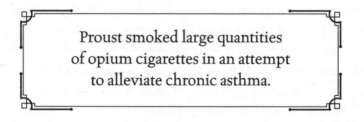

Proust smoked large quantities of opium cigarettes in an attempt to alleviate chronic asthma.

The circumstances of the novel's composition are almost as famous as those two significant events that occur within it. Retreating to his cork-lined room (so as to block out noise from the bustling and increasingly fast-moving outside world), Proust effectively became a night owl, lying in till late in the afternoon and then working through much of the night. He ate very little beside a croissant or two for breakfast (if you can call a five o'clock evening repast 'breakfast'), though he did sometimes dine out. On one notable occasion, in May 1922, he dined with a number of fellow modernists, including James Joyce, Picasso and Stravinsky. Joyce and Proust spent the meal discussing their ailments, before eventually admitting that they hadn't read each other's work.

## ✧ A Literary Pilgrimage ✧

'Stream of consciousness'. You may have heard the term, but where did it come from, and what does it mean? The answers are perhaps surprising, and lead us to a largely forgotten modernist writer whom Virginia Woolf, among others, praised.

It is often claimed that the term 'stream of consciousness' was coined by the philosopher and psychologist William James, brother of novelist Henry James, in his book *The Principles of Psychology* (1890). Sure enough, James himself gives us this impression when he uses the phrase when discussing conscious thought: 'A "river" or a "stream" are the metaphors by which it is most naturally described. *In talking of it hereafter, let's call it the stream of thought, consciousness, or subjective life.*' But this was not the first use of the phrase by a psychologist, and James was actually borrowing (to put it politely) an expression that had been coined some years earlier. The real coiner was a forgotten psychologist named Alexander Bain, who used 'stream of consciousness' in his 1855 work *The Senses and the Intellect*. This shows that 'stream of consciousness', although associated with modernist writing of the early twentieth century, was a mid-Victorian coinage rather than a late-Victorian, or proto-modernist, metaphor.

The term 'stream of consciousness' is most commonly associated with the writing of Virginia Woolf and James Joyce, those key modernist novelists (pleasingly, Woolf and Joyce were born in the same year, and also died in the same year; they also both wrote novels set over just one day in mid-June, *Ulysses* and *Mrs Dalloway*). In their work, characters' thoughts are presented not in a logical and ordered fashion, but as a 'stream' or flow of ideas and impressions, with one succeeding another without necessarily making logical sense. In other words, how most of us 'think' on a daily basis. But in fact the word was first applied to another modernist writer, whose name is not as well known as Woolf's or Joyce's.

Dorothy Richardson (1873–1957) wrote a long sequence of novels called *Pilgrimage*, published in thirteen volumes between 1915 and 1967 and perhaps modelled on Proust's multi-novel sequence *In Search of Lost Time*. It's a difficult and frustrating work, obsessed with tiny details such as towel rails and the pattern in the carpet to an almost dizzying (or coma-inducing) degree. *Pilgrimage* follows Miriam Henderson as she grows to maturity, eventually becoming a successful writer (as Richardson's detractors might quip, something her creator never quite manages). What sets this sequence apart from other modernist works is the relentless attention to detail: the patterns in that carpet, the state of that towel rail, the noises coming from the people in the flat next door. For some, such a level of detail is refreshing and reflects real life; for others, it is merely dull, for the reader can never be sure what is significant for the story (if that is quite the word here) and what is not. But then that is partly what Richardson is inviting us to question: what is 'significant', and what is 'story', anyway? How close can fiction ever come to conveying the humdrum realities of everyday life?

One of the distinctive features of Richardson's prose is the new style. It was this that led May Sinclair to apply the term 'stream of consciousness' to a literary work – the first time this had been done. (It was in a review of Richardson's work in a magazine called *The Egoist* in 1918.) Woolf herself remarked in 1923 that Richardson 'has invented, or, if she has not invented, developed and applied to her own uses, a sentence which we might call the psychological sentence of the feminine gender'. But Richardson herself didn't like the term 'stream of consciousness', instead preferring to see her style as a form of *immersion*, which implies an attempt to capture the simultaneous and multifaceted nature of thought and experience rather than a desire to convey something moving in one direction like a 'stream'.

So, although 'stream of consciousness' more readily conjures up James Joyce and Virginia Woolf in the annals of modernist fiction, we should not forget Dorothy Richardson, despite her own reservations about the applicability of the term to her own work. Next time you catch your thoughts wandering, think of Richardson as well as Woolf.

## ✧ Before Gatsby ✧

F. Scott Fitzgerald might be surprised that his third novel is now his most popular. *The Great Gatsby* sold no more than 25,000 copies in his lifetime; it has now sold over 25 million. The novel's evocation of 1920s America and its critique of the American Dream has helped to ensure its place among the great American novels, but it was outsold at the time by *This Side of Paradise*, Fitzgerald's first novel, published in 1920. *This Side of Paradise* is a response to the First World War and its emotional and psychological fallout. Ironically, the novel took its title from a poem by Rupert Brooke, one of

Virginia Woolf's fellow 'Bloomsberries' (as the Bloomsbury Group were sometimes disparagingly known), who would become known for patriotic war poems such as 'The Soldier' and who would die during the early years of the war.

*This Side of Paradise* was written at speed for that noblest of motives: to try to impress a woman. Fitzgerald and his girlfriend Zelda had been an item for a short while, but she broke up with him. He wrote the novel in order to become a successful writer and win her back. It worked: the novel was published on 26 March, and before the month was out the first print run of 3,000 copies had sold out and Zelda had agreed to marry him.

F. Scott Fitzgerald's full name was Francis Scott Key Fitzgerald – he was named after Francis Scott Key, the man who wrote the lyrics to the American national anthem, 'The Star-Spangled Banner', and a distant relation of the family. Fitzgerald was born in Minnesota in 1896, and completed just four novels: *This Side of Paradise* (1920), *The Beautiful and Damned* (1922), *The Great Gatsby* (1925) and *Tender is the Night* (1934). A fifth novel was left unfinished at his death: for many years this was known as *The Last Tycoon*, though it is more properly known by the full title *The Love of the Last Tycoon*, in keeping with Fitzgerald's preferred choice of title.

> F. Scott Fitzgerald's father was the first cousin, once removed, of Mary Surratt, a woman hanged in 1865 for conspiring to assassinate Abraham Lincoln.

While in Paris with his wife Zelda in the 1920s, Fitzgerald became friends with numerous other writers, most notably Ernest Hemingway. Hemingway considered Zelda 'insane'; she would be hospitalized for schizophrenia in the 1930s. He also thought she was a bad influence on Fitzgerald, encouraging her husband to drink when he should have been working. Zelda returned the compliment by describing Hemingway's early novel *The Sun Also Rises* as being about three things: 'bullfighting, bull-slinging, and bullshitting'. In 1936 Fitzgerald did attempt to 'dry out', hiring a nurse called Dorothy Richardson (not she of *Pilgrimage* non-fame) and drawing up a list of his must-read books for her. (These included three books by Marcel Proust, the plays of Oscar Wilde, and *War and Peace*, among others.)

Fitzgerald is credited, in the *Oxford English Dictionary*, with the first citations of the words 'T-shirt', 'daiquiri' (a cocktail containing rum and lime, named after a region of Cuba), 'stinko' (slang meaning 'of a very low standard'), and even 'wicked' (as in 'excellent' or 'remarkable'). With the exception of 'stinko' (which comes from a letter of 1924), all of these early uses of these words are found in Fitzgerald's first novel, *This Side of Paradise*.

## ⟡ Flushed Away ⟡

One of Virginia Woolf's first published writings was an obituary for the family dog, Shag. She would continue to write about animals, returning to dogs for an overlooked but marvellous book, *Flush: A Biography*, published in 1933. *Flush*, like Woolf's earlier book *Orlando*, is described in the book's subtitle as 'a biography' but is really a novel, though it takes its cue from a real-life subject.

> As a young girl, Virginia Woolf had pets including a marmoset, a squirrel, and a mouse she named Jacobi.

The courtship and subsequent marriage between Elizabeth Barrett and Robert Browning is one of the great Victorian love stories. The two poets – she an established name in Victorian letters, he a virtually unknown writer at the time – sent a series of romantic letters to each other before they met; soon after they did eventually meet and clap eyes on each other, they married. After that, their son 'Pen' later recalled, they never wrote to each other again because they were never apart. In 1930 a play about the courtship, *The Barretts of Wimpole Street*, was staged. The story of the Brownings' courtship may have been in Woolf's mind because of this play. Whatever it was that gave her the idea, Woolf decided to write a short work about this famous literary love story, but with an unusual focus: *Flush* is told from the perspective of Elizabeth Barrett's pet dog.

*Flush* is among Woolf's funniest works, in both senses of the word: charmingly odd but also gently humorous. The book was conceived partly as a bit of light relief after Woolf completed her 1931 novel *The Waves*, which is somewhat short on laughs. Although *Flush* is an altogether lighter book than Woolf's other titles, it touches upon similar issues, albeit from a slightly different angle. Woolf's nephew and biographer Quentin Bell went so far as to claim that *Flush* is not simply a book written by an admirer of dogs – it's a book written by someone who would love to *be* a dog.

What's more, although it's often downplayed by Woolf scholars, *Flush* shares something with her more famous 1928 novel *Orlando* (also, like *Flush*, subtitled *A Biography*): it's a light-hearted but also purposeful riposte to the kinds of biography Woolf had encountered growing up in the Victorian era. Woolf's friend Lytton Strachey, another member of the Bloomsbury Group, wrote a popular book, *Eminent Victorians* (1918), poking fun at the Victorian approach to biography, as well as at the Victorians themselves. Woolf had first-hand experience of all this: her father, Sir Leslie Stephen, was the founder of the *Dictionary of National Biography*. A biography, not of one of the great poets of the Victorian age, but of her cocker spaniel, can be read as a send-up of the idea of writing the lives of great men and women. What, for all that, about their pets?

## ✧ Consequences ✧

Another Bloomsberry, associated with Woolf and her friends, was the economist John Maynard Keynes. Although he is without doubt one of the key figures – perhaps *the* key figure – in twentieth-century economics, he studied mathematics at Cambridge and his only formal training in economics was an eight-week postgraduate course he undertook before entering the civil service. Despite this, he would be appointed to a lectureship in economics at his old college, King's, at the fresh young age of twenty-five.

Keynes was a progressive in all sorts of ways. In 1925 he gave a talk advocating contraception to a summer school at Cambridge. This was a daring issue to broach at the time: a young student, the precocious critic and poet William Empson, would be expelled from Cambridge four years later when condoms were found in his possession. It is not for his daring prophylactic talk that Keynes is best remembered, but for his work in economics, especially the 1936 book *The General Theory of Employment, Interest and Money*, which few people outside of economics can say they fully understand (not everyone *within* economics does either).

But Keynes first came to the world's attention following the publication in 1919 of his book *The Economic Consequences of the Peace*. This short book came out of his observation of the Paris Peace Talks earlier in the same year. Unhappy with the terms drawn up in the Treaty of Versailles, Keynes withdrew from the Peace Talks in disgust. Europe was starving and on the brink of self-destruction, yet nobody wanted to address that fact. The reparation demands drawn up for Germany were deemed far too punitive by Keynes. Prophetically, he warned that punishing Germany too harshly after the war, and seeking to limit its economic power, would lead to further unrest and conflict in the future.

*The Economic Consequences of the Peace* meant that Keynes's name was more or less mud in establishment circles for the next twenty years. Nobody liked to admit, as National Socialism took over Germany and Europe was once again brought to the brink of war, that Keynes had been right. He was often right.

But being right doesn't always make you popular.

But his importance in modern economics, for all that, is indisputable. As well as being probably the most important economist of the twentieth century, Keynes would leave one other substantial legacy. Always a prominent supporter of the arts, he was instrumental in setting up the Arts Council of Great Britain during the Second World War.

## ✥ Indifferent Voices ✥

One enthusiastic reader of *The Economic Consequences of the Peace* was a bowler-hatted employee of Lloyds Bank in London, who had published a couple of volumes of poems. They had both had modest print runs: the first volume, published in 1917 in an edition of 500 copies, would not sell out for five years. But this quiet bank clerk was also becoming known among the Bloomsberries – including Keynes and Woolf – and was about to write a poem that would change the poetic landscape for ever.

The poet's name was T. S. Eliot and the poem, *The Waste Land*, is perhaps the most important poem of the twentieth century. It captured the post-war mood in numerous ways: the sense of loss, of despair and alienation, the notion that life had become one long repetitive treadmill of mechanical routine. Indeed, the dull routine of the daily grind looms large in Eliot's poem: the typist with her food laid out in tins for when she gets in from work, the crowds of commuters travelling over London Bridge, the empty sexual encounters between Lil and her husband Albert, and between the typist and her spotty young beau. In the last of these examples, this repetitiveness is neatly encapsulated by the gramophone: for the first time, one can play the same song over and over again ad nauseam, rather than having to hear music 'live' or not at all. We've gained something from this, but we've also lost something, Eliot seems to be saying. Life has lost its purpose, its electrifying excitement, its sense of a deeper meaning.

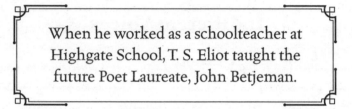

When he worked as a schoolteacher at Highgate School, T. S. Eliot taught the future Poet Laureate, John Betjeman.

But beneath such strains of ennui – what Eliot himself called 'aboulia' or lack of will – there are other, more surprising undercurrents. Keynes's book appears to have found its way into several aspects of *The Waste Land*, as the critic Eleanor Cook argued. Where Keynes talks about a 'Carthaginian peace', Eliot's poem parallels modern-day London (whose iconic bridge is 'falling down', as the appropriated nursery rhyme has it) with ancient Carthage. The implication is that all great empires inevitably fall, and that London, now in the grip of irresponsible financiers (there's a thought!), is next on the list. This time it will be financial ruin (think of all those merchants in Eliot's poem, alongside other financial references to things like profit and loss) that does for the great city: London will be brought down by bankers.

The poem started out as a jumble of unconnected sketches

and lyrics, given the rather unpromising working title 'He Do the Police in Different Voices', after a line from Dickens's *Our Mutual Friend*. It was thanks to Ezra Pound, Eliot's friend and fellow American expatriate in Europe, that *The Waste Land* became the poem we now read. Pound took his red pen to Eliot's early drafts, halved the poem's length, and gave it a loose sense of cohesion. When the poem was completed, Pound had just two words of begrudging admiration for his friend: '*Complimenti*, bitch!' Eliot had three words in response, which adorn the title page of the poem: 'For Ezra Pound'. To this dedication he appended three additional words in Italian: '*Il miglior fabbro*' ('the better craftsman'). Certainly, Pound's craftsmanship had played a key role in making *The Waste Land* what it is.

The poem quickly became a landmark in twentieth-century poetry, and it went on to influence everyone from novelists to musicians. As a young undergraduate at Oxford, Harold Acton recited it out of a megaphone across Christ Church Meadow. Evelyn Waugh later borrowed this scene for his novel *Brideshead Revisited*. Not everyone has been impressed by Eliot's poem, though. The Queen Mother was once in the audience for a special reading of *The Waste Land*, by Eliot himself, at Windsor Castle. Reportedly unimpressed by Eliot and by his work, she later misremembered his poem's title as 'The Desert'.

## ✥ Mapping the City ✥

Here's a question. Can you name a road in the City of London? Any road you like. What about Grub Street, the street that for a long time was synonymous with hack writers?

Or Threadneedle Street, home of the Bank of England? Or how about King William Street, mentioned in Eliot's *The Waste Land*? Or perhaps Gropecunt Lane, which provides the *Oxford English Dictionary* with its earliest citation for a certain naughty word? None of those is a road. Technically, there isn't a single road in the City of London.

Admittedly this is a technicality, which turns on a bit of semantics, or rather a couple of bits. First, the 'City of London' is different from the much larger city we call London: the former refers to the central district, otherwise known as the 'Square Mile', and there are no 'roads' in this part of the capital. This is because historically a 'road' was a tree-lined avenue whereas a 'street' was not. By the Middle Ages, there wasn't much room for trees in the bustling Square Mile, so all of the various alleys and lanes that make up the City of London are considered to be various types of thoroughfares, but not one is a *road*. So, now we know.

In 1935, a young artist named Phyllis Pearsall supposedly came up with the idea of drawing a detailed and updated road map of the city – the whole city, not just 'the City' – when she got lost on her way to a party. The existing maps weren't much help, and she spotted a gap in the market. She spent a year walking some 3,000 miles around London, making a note of over 23,000 streets, at the end of which exertions she had produced the iconic *London A-Z* – at least, so the story goes. Some say we should treat this origin story with a pinch of salt, arguing that Pearsall simply updated existing maps. Indeed, there were numerous road maps of London before the *A-Z* – *Bartholomew's Reference Atlas of London and Suburbs* had been published in 1908 – and, handily, Pearsall's own father, Alexander Gross, was a cartographer who had drawn up London maps which are strikingly similar to the later *A-Z*.

But what the *A-Z* had going for it was that it was pocket-sized and easy to read, as well as pretty comprehensive. It was published at Pearsall's own expense in 1936, but the problem was that none of the bookshops would touch it at first. Eventually, the persistent Pearsall convinced W. H. Smith to take some copies, and demand for the book quickly grew. To date, sales are reckoned to be at around the 65-million mark. It is still being published, despite the increasing popularity of satellite navigation systems, and many London cabbies still use Pearsall's book to help them obtain 'the Knowledge' they need to acquire in order to drive a taxi in the capital.

However, the *A-Z* does contain mistakes. Well, of a sort: over the years a number of inaccuracies have been *deliberately* inserted as a way of catching out mapmakers who plagiarize the map. The first of these was Bartlett Place, a fake name for a real street whose actual name is Broadway Walk.

A similar thing occurs with dictionaries. The *New Oxford American Dictionary* contains an entry for the word 'esquivalience', a plausible-sounding noun denoting 'the wilful avoidance of one's official responsibilities'. Aptly, the word was made up by one of the editors, Christine Lindberg, to catch out plagiarists.

## ⟡ From 'A' to 'Zythum' ⟡

Just over a century after Samuel Johnson published his dictionary, work began on an enterprise that would dwarf even the good doctor's lexicographical achievement. Begun in 1857, the first volume would appear twenty-seven years later under the title *A New English Dictionary on Historical*

*Principles; Founded Mainly on the Materials Collected by The Philological Society.* Later it would become known as the *Oxford English Dictionary.* It covers everything from 'a' (as in the indefinite article) through to 'zythum' (a kind of malt beer in ancient Egypt) – a true A-Z of the English language. (The cartoon-inspired onomatopoeic word 'zzz' – denoting the snoring sound of someone snatching forty winks – hasn't made it past the gatekeepers of the *OED* yet, though 'zizz', which has the same meaning, has.)

Right from the beginning, the undertaking attracted some prestigious literary names. The first editor of what later became the *Oxford English Dictionary* was Herbert Coleridge, grandson of the poet Samuel Taylor Coleridge. J. R. R. Tolkien's first job after the First World War was working on entries for the letter W. More recently, a young Julian Barnes's first graduate job was as a researcher for the *OED*, tracking down the etymologies of words in the C–G letter range.

'Aardvark' isn't the first word in the dictionary – the *OED* lists several words before it including 'a' (the indefinite article previously mentioned), 'aa' (an old word for a stream), 'aal' (a type of mulberry), 'aam' (a unit of liquid measurement), 'aandblom' (a species of South African flower) and 'aapa' (a term for an older sister, originating in Asia). The fact that 'aardvark' isn't even among the first five entries gives a sense of the scale of the dictionary and just how much more comprehensive it was than previous attempts to document the language. If laid end to end, the typescript for the first edition would have stretched from London to Manchester.

> Work on the *OED* was not without its setbacks:
> at one point the entire record of entries for
> the letter 'Q' went missing, later turning
> up safe and sound in Loughborough.

The real driving force behind the *Oxford English Dictionary* was James Murray. Under his leadership, the dictionary was compiled, edited and published, with the final instalment coming out in 1928, some forty-four years after the first part had appeared. Given the extent of the project, this is not bad going. Work on the definitive dictionary of the Welsh language began in 1921 but was not completed until 2002; while the first volume of the official Dutch dictionary came out in 1864, the fortieth and final volume did not appear until 1998.

## ⟡ Four-Letter Controversies ⟡

The stronger swear words could not be found in English dictionaries until the 1960s: the *Penguin English Dictionary* admitted 'fuck' in 1965, 170 years since it had last been included in an English lexicon. The *Oxford English Dictionary* followed suit in 1972, though intriguingly the word had sort of been there from the start, in 'windfucker', a word that had appeared in the first edition back in the 1920s. 'Windfucker' is another word for the kestrel, like 'windhover' – though the former would admittedly have given that poem by Gerard Manley Hopkins a somewhat different feel.

Part of the reason for this sea change in the 1960s was a response to the events of 1960: specifically, the *Chatterley* trial. Following the Obscene Publications Act in 1959, it became possible to publish a dirty book in the UK as long as one could prove the book in question had 'redeeming social merit'. (How one went about proving that is another matter.) The book had originally been privately printed in 1928 but was not officially available in either Britain or the United States for over thirty years: despite their reputation for prudishness, America actually published the novel first, the year before it appeared in Britain. A common perception about D. H. Lawrence's *Lady Chatterley's Lover* is that it was the book's sexual content that led to its being banned. The descriptions of what Lawrence calls 'this sex business' and 'orgasmic satisfaction' didn't help, but it was actually more the use of four-letter words than the erotic descriptions of lovemaking that landed Penguin in court for publishing it in 1960. A year before Penguin brought out *Chatterley*, a UK publisher had successfully published Vladimir Nabokov's *Lolita*, which has a paedophile as a narrator but, you know, had the redeeming feature of being sans expletives. The prosecuting lawyer, Mervyn Griffith-Jones, counted up the offensive words: '30 "fucks" or "fuckings"; 14 "cunts"; 13 "balls"; 6 each of "shit" and "arse"; 4 "cocks" and 3 "piss"'. Of course, to itemize these offending examples Griffith-Jones had to read them out in court: the swearing on the Bible wasn't the only swearing that went on at the *Chatterley* trial.

The book chronicles Constance Chatterley's affair with the gamekeeper Oliver Mellors (though her first affair in the book is actually with a writer named Michaelis), but it was as much the language of the novel as the scenes of a sexual nature that raised the hackles of the puritans. The arguments made by the prosecution now seem pitifully quaint, if not a little puritanical. It was Griffith-Jones who asked the jury the memorable question: 'Is it a book that you would even wish your wife or your servants to read?' But what is more surprising is the long line of – often surprising – people who queued up to speak in defence of the novel. The Bishop of Woolwich, John Robinson, described the adulterous affair between Lady Constance Chatterley and her gamekeeper Mellors as 'an act of holy communion'. What Lawrence would have made of this (he died in 1930) one cannot but wonder.

Despite this impressive list of supporters, the trial lasted nearly a fortnight before Penguin was acquitted. The novel that Lawrence, over thirty years before, had originally drafted under the title 'John Thomas and Lady Jane' (i.e. penis and vagina) now went on to sell by the barrowload.

Surprisingly, though, the Chatterley trial didn't mark the end of such prosecutions. There were still plenty of books that were, so Middle England maintained, out to corrupt the country, without the saving grace of possessing redeeming social merit. In 1964, the London bookseller Ralph Gold found himself in the dock for selling John Cleland's *Fanny Hill*, a book that had first been published some 215 years earlier but had only recently appeared in unexpurgated form. He lost, and the publishers of the unabridged *Fanny* decided against an appeal. Although *Chatterley* was a watershed of sorts, publishers continued to think twice about disseminating books containing too much of the sexy stuff. *Fanny Hill* wouldn't be back on bookshelves in all her glory until the end of the decade.

## ✧ A Giant . . . Beetle? ✧

If literature has a patron saint of bureaucracy, or rather the ways in which administrative and legal procedures can attack our very humanity and can be used as weapons against us, it is Franz Kafka (1883–1924). Fittingly, he worked for many years in that most officious of office jobs, as an insurance clerk. He even has his own adjective, 'Kafkaesque', which conveys the sense of bewilderment and alienation that we often experience in the face of bureaucratic procedures and state surveillance. It's hardly surprising, then, that he has been hailed as a prophet of both the police state (later taken up by George Orwell in *Nineteen Eighty-Four*) and, more eerily, the Holocaust.

As a writer and a man, Kafka was always the outsider. Early in life he made a 'writer's pact' with the Devil and resolved effectively to shut himself off from any real intimacy with other people. The writer's life is so often a lonely one. Although he was involved with several women, he never married. He evidently had an interest in sex, but he would always watch from the sidelines: he would attend nudist camps but refused to drop his trousers. (This quickly earned him the sobriquet 'The Man in the Swimming Trunks'.)

> Kafka is credited with inventing the hard hat, as part of his day job working as an accident claims insurance clerk.

It's small wonder, then, that he appears to have identified with the protagonist of his short masterpiece, *The Metamorphosis*. It was published in German in 1915, with the first English translation appearing in 1933. The book tells of a travelling salesman, Gregor Samsa, who wakes one day to find that he has transformed into a giant insect. This surreal turn of events leads to his being ostracized by his nearest and dearest: nobody likes having a gigantic beetle around the house, making a mess.

I say 'insect' and 'beetle' because the one thing people know about Kafka's novella is that Gregor turns into an insect. Many English translations use the word in the book's famous opening line, which pulls the reader up short by immediately revealing the fact of Gregor's transformation. But the German *Ungeziefer* does not lend itself easily to translation. It roughly denotes any unclean being or creature, and 'bug' is a more accurate rendering of the original into English – though even 'bug' doesn't quite do it, since (in English anyway) it still suggests an insect, or at least some sort of creepy-crawly. For this reason, some translators reach for the word *vermin*, which is probably closer to the German original. Certainly at no point does Kafka's narrator say that Gregor is a beetle, although that hasn't stopped numerous illustrators from drawing him as such. (Kafka did use the word *Insekt* in his correspondence discussing the book, but ordered that the creature must not be drawn at any cost.) The point – as with much of Kafka – is that we are not supposed to know the precise *thing* into which Gregor has metamorphosed. The vagueness is part of the effect: Gregor is any and every unworthy or downtrodden creature, shunned by those closest to him. Much as those who wish to denigrate a particular group of people – immigrants, foreigners, a socio-economic underclass –

often reach for words like 'cockroaches' or 'vermin', so Gregor's transformation physically enacts and literalizes such emotive propaganda. Shortly after his death, the race to which Kafka belonged – the Jewish race – would be described as 'vermin' by the Nazis.

Like D. H. Lawrence, Kafka was one of the generation of modernists who would be claimed by tuberculosis while still in their prime (Katherine Mansfield was another). As he lay dying, Kafka asked his friend Max Brod to burn his unpublished work. Thankfully, Brod refused to comply. If he had, we wouldn't have *The Trial* or *The Castle* (unfinished though it was), which, with *The Metamorphosis*, form Kafka's crowning literary achievement. Another book to escape the flames was *Amerika*, the first novel Kafka wrote, which was only first published three years after his death.

## ✧ The First Robots ✧

Here's a question for you: when did the word 'robot' first enter the English language? The most common definition of 'robot' is the one provided by the *Oxford English Dictionary*: 'An intelligent artificial being typically made of metal and resembling in some way a human or other animal.' But the story of how the word came to have this meaning is a curious one.

'Robot' makes its debut in the English language, perhaps surprisingly, during the Victorian age: the first citation is from 1839. But it doesn't refer to the humanoid machines of a million science-fiction novels and films written and made since, but rather to a 'central European system of serfdom, by which a tenant's rent was paid in forced labour or service' (*OED*). This word came to English via the German, though the word ultimately derives from the Czech *robota* meaning 'forced labour' or 'slavery'. Not a very pleasant etymology; though the Austrian empire banned slavery in 1848, which is something.

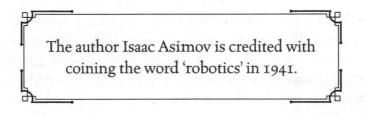

The author Isaac Asimov is credited with coining the word 'robotics' in 1941.

The modern meaning of the word 'robot' has its origins in a 1920 play by the Czech writer Karel Čapek. The play, titled *R. U. R. (Rossum's Universal Robots)*, begins in a factory that manufactures artificial people, the 'universal robots' of the play's title. The robots are designed to serve humans and work for them, but the robots eventually turn on their masters, wiping out the human race (shades, or rather a foreshadowing, of *The Terminator* here). This sense of 'robot' is taken from the earlier one defined above – namely, the Czech for 'slave worker' or 'drudge'. Karel Čapek himself didn't coin the word. As we've already seen, it was in existence before he wrote his play. But nor did Čapek come up with the idea of taking the word 'robot' and using it to describe the man-made droids that feature in his play. He originally called them *labori*, from the Latin for 'work', but it was his brother, Josef Čapek, who suggested *roboti*. Josef, himself a gifted artist, would later write a volume of poems from the Bergen-Belsen concentration camp in which he was interned. In April 1945, just weeks before the end of the war, he became one of the 6 million Jews who were murdered in Hitler's Final Solution.

Curiously, the robots that feature in *Rossum's Universal Robots* aren't really robots – at least, not if we're being picky and technical. They are closer to androids or cyborgs than robots. The difference is that androids and cyborgs resemble real human beings, whereas robots don't. Because the droids in Čapek's play look very much like us, the first 'robots' in literature to be so named were, in a sense, misnamed. Or, because Čapek got there first, we are the ones who've been 'misusing' his word ever since. Except, as we've seen, it wasn't his word.

In 1938, Čapek's play was adapted by the BBC, and became the first piece of television science fiction ever to be broadcast.

## ✧ Dear Kitty ✧

There is a persistent story about a bad stage adaptation of Anne Frank's diary, which involved an incompetent lead actress in the title role who fluffed her opening lines, with the performance getting worse as the show wore on. The audience had become so bored and disgruntled that, when the Nazi officers showed up at the house, an audience member yelled out, 'She's in the attic!' The story is, like many such stories, legend: none of the various accounts of it can agree on who the actress playing Frank was, or even when this theatrical adaptation was staged, so it's unlikely the famous heckle ever occurred.

Kafka's three siblings would perish in Nazi concentration camps. Karel Čapek's brother did too. Primo Levi, author of

*The Periodic Table*, survived the Holocaust and wrote about the horrors that he had seen while imprisoned at Auschwitz. And, perhaps most famously of all, the young Jewish girl Anne Frank died in one of Hitler's concentration camps in 1945. Along with Samuel Pepys's diary from nearly three centuries before, Anne's *Diary of a Young Girl* is probably the most famous diary ever kept.

Anne received an autograph book for her thirteenth birthday, but chose to start using it as a diary instead, penning her first entry on 14 June 1942. Rather than begin each entry 'Dear diary', she named the diary 'Kitty', as though she were writing letters to a pen pal; many of the entries in her diary thus begin 'Dear Kitty'. The diary chronicles two years in her adolescent life as Anne and her family live in hiding in Amsterdam, never knowing when their hiding place will be discovered and they will be taken off to a concentration camp. That day came in August 1944; Anne died of typhus in Bergen-Belsen around six months later, not long before the end of the war.

The circumstances surrounding the final few years of Anne's brief life clearly help to explain the diary's especial fascination for millions of readers. The sense of fear and uncertainty, but also the determination to survive and carry on, pervades the diary: humour and solidarity temper the anxiety and terror of expecting the wrong knock at the door at any moment. The rooms where Anne and her family concealed themselves were located in a secret annexe at the top of her father's business premises; the door leading to their hiding place was secreted behind a movable bookcase.

Anne's father Otto survived the horrors of the Final Solution and published his daughter's diary in Amsterdam in 1947. Getting an English translation into print proved trickier. It was rejected by ten publishers before it eventually appeared in 1952. One editor wrote: 'The girl doesn't, it seems to me, have a special perception or feeling which would lift that book above the "curiosity" level.' It is now thought to have sold in excess of 30 million copies in over sixty different languages. Curiosity, it would seem, is far more widespread than that editor realized.

## ⋄ Beloved Country ⋄

Published in 1987, Toni Morrison's *Beloved* begins with a controversial epigraph of just four words: 'Sixty Million and more'. The controversy lies in the perceived relation between 'sixty million' and 'six million' – respectively, the number of African slaves who are estimated to have died as a result of the Atlantic slave trade, and the number of Jewish people murdered in the Holocaust. In drawing a suggestive link between the atrocities of the Holocaust and the slave trade, Morrison got people's attention. Had more recent tragedies led people to forget about the horrors of slavery?

*Beloved* offers a powerful and impassioned account of the lives of African slaves living in the United States during the nineteenth century. It's somewhat different from Harriet Beecher Stowe's treatment of the subject some 130 years earlier, though both novels have been criticized by their detractors as overly sentimental. Focusing on a mother and daughter who had escaped a life of slavery a few years before the outbreak of the American Civil War, *Beloved* moves between pre-war (or 'antebellum') and post-war ('postbellum') America. The novel's protagonist, Sethe, is visited by a fellow slave from the plantation she worked on nearly twenty years ago; the arrival of this ghost from the past prompts a series of reminiscences about Sethe's earlier life as a slave.

From an early age, Morrison's world revolved around books. Born Chloe Ardelia Wofford in Ohio in 1931, she was the only black child in her first-grade class at school – and the only child who could read. This early aptitude for reading led to her studying at university, and then staying on to undertake a Master's degree on the work of William Faulkner and Virginia Woolf. She then taught English at university, before becoming an editor for several publishing houses. During this time she was instrumental in getting young black authors into print – including, ultimately, herself. Her first novel, *The Bluest Eye*, appeared in 1970.

> When *Beloved* was nominated for, but failed to win, the National Book Award, forty-eight African-American writers and critics signed a letter of protest.

Like Alice Walker's *The Color Purple*, filmed to huge acclaim by Steven Spielberg in 1985, *Beloved* revealed the truth about the suffering and hardships endured by African-American people in America. In particular, these popular and critically acclaimed novels gave a voice to African-American women writers. Morrison has said that she wrote her first novel because she wanted to read it. Millions of other people have wanted to read her, too. *Beloved* got the recognition it deserved when it won Morrison the Pulitzer Prize.

Morrison's many high-profile admirers have included some perhaps unlikely figures, among them Marlon Brando, who was a huge fan of her work. He would reportedly ring her up and recite his favourite passages from her novels down the line.

## ❖ Dinomania ❖

Which novel is being described here? Published in 1984, it centres on the scientific idea of recreating dinosaurs from DNA fragments found in fossils. A number of dinosaurs are reconstructed, including a fearsome *Tyrannosaurus rex*. The novel features a whole theme park filled with dinosaurs. A film adaptation was released in 1993. Got the answer? I'm not describing *Jurassic Park* – although all of the above could apply equally to Michael Crichton's novel, more or less, with the exception of the publication date: Crichton's book was published in 1990.

Instead, the 1984 novel being described above is *Carnosaur*, written by the Australian author Harry Adam Knight, the pseudonym of John Brosnan. The book did not sell particularly well, and Roger Corman's 1993 adaptation did poorly at the box office – losing out to Steven Spielberg's blockbuster film version of Crichton's book. Brosnan himself described the film *Carnosaur* as 'crap' – though he added that it was '*interesting* crap'. I agree that it is interesting, not least because it provides a neat complement to Crichton's more famous vision of dinosaurs run amok. *Carnosaur* centres on a 'dinosaur zoo' and is set in England rather than on a tropical island, but the main thrust of the story – cloned dinosaurs wreaking havoc – is the same as in *Jurassic Park*.

Both *Carnosaur* and *Jurassic Park* owe a huge debt to Sir Arthur Conan Doyle. More than this, the similarities between Crichton and Conan Doyle are curious: both trained in medicine, both wrote novels called *The Lost World*, both wrote novels set in the fourteenth century (*The White Company* and its prequel *Sir Nigel* in the case of Conan Doyle, and *Timeline* in Crichton's). *Jurassic Park*, Crichton's most commercially successful novel, was effectively a clever updating of the premise of Conan Doyle's 1912 classic *The Lost World*. In Conan Doyle's novel, Professor Challenger and a band of intrepid explorers go to South America in search of a rainforest plateau that has somehow remained untouched by the modern world, and as a result is still a habitat for prehistoric creatures, including dinosaurs. The *Guardian* obituary for Crichton in 2008 likened him to Conan Doyle, and in some ways Crichton can be seen as Doyle's heir.

Crichton is a prime example of the stratospheric bestsellerdom that a handful of authors enjoyed during the late twentieth century, thanks largely to a string of successful film adaptations of their work (Stephen King is another). Crichton had been a successful author for two decades before he published *Jurassic Park*. He published the most influential of his early novels, *The Andromeda Strain*, in 1969. Pleasingly, when the novel was adapted into a film two years later, Crichton was given a tour of the set by a young Steven Spielberg, who was on his first day at work as a film director. Twenty-two years later, of course, Spielberg would direct the feature-film adaptation of *Jurassic Park*.

Crichton was also the author of *Westworld*. The 1973 film adaptation of the book, which Crichton also directed, was the first-ever film to use CGI.

# ❖ From Printing to Surfing ❖

CGI may have first been used back in 1973, but the kind of technical wizardry found in modern film was still a few decades away. The World Wide Web, too, was yet to be born – though the internet (which is not exactly synonymous with the Web) had already taken its first tentative steps.

Nevertheless, one man had already imagined the World Wide Web of the future. He wasn't a science-fiction writer but a Canadian philosopher of 'communication theory' named Marshall McLuhan. In his pioneering 1962 book *The Gutenberg Galaxy*, McLuhan predicted the World Wide Web nearly thirty years before it was invented.

The central argument of *The Gutenberg Galaxy* is that the development of technologies such as movable type and mass-printing had not simply changed the way we read, write or buy books: they had brought about a change in the very ways we think, the ways we experience the world. McLuhan also speculated on what the next big development in technology might be, predicting that it will include television as part of its content, and will feature a computer as a tool for research and communication, giving every user access to an unprecedented amount of information, all just a few clicks away.

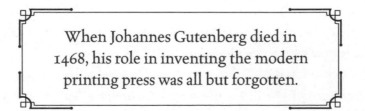

When Johannes Gutenberg died in 1468, his role in inventing the modern printing press was all but forgotten.

The metaphor of 'surfing' the internet was McLuhan's creation, too. In the same book, McLuhan writes poetically of the philosopher Martin Heidegger surfboarding along on the electronic wave as triumphantly as Descartes had ridden the mechanical wave of the previous great technological revolution – that is, the one initiated by Gutenberg's printing press.

McLuhan had a gift for phrasemaking and is perhaps best known for coining the phrase 'global village' to describe the ways in which new electronic technologies – chief among them the as yet unknown and uninvented World Wide Web – would, in social and psychological terms, make the world a lot smaller. Indeed, McLuhan was something of a sloganeer: Timothy Leary also credited McLuhan with originating the slogan 'turn on, tune in, drop out', which Leary popularized as a maxim for the 1960s counterculture. In 1967 McLuhan wrote a book titled *The Medium is the Massage*, the title being a twist on another of his popular phrases, 'the medium is the message'.

Marshall McLuhan thought readers should turn to page 69 of any book to determine whether it's any good. The modernist writer Ford Madox Ford had offered similar advice, but had recommended page 99 rather than 69. So, with that in mind, let us proceed to our ninety-ninth stop on this whistle-stop tour of the library.

## ✦ New Intelligence ✦

On 3 April 1995, an Australian software engineer named John Wainwright did something that nobody had ever done before: he went online and ordered a book with the rather unpromising title *Fluid Concepts and Creative Analogies* by Douglas Hofstadter. In doing so, he became the first-ever customer to buy a book from Amazon.com.

Hofstadter is best known for his 1979 book *Gödel, Escher, Bach*, which discusses shared concepts found across such apparently disparate subjects and disciplines as mathematics, art and music. That book won him a Pulitzer Prize. *Fluid Concepts*, in some ways a continuation of that earlier work, is not as well known to the non-academic world. Subtitled *Computer Models of the Fundamental Mechanisms of Thought*, Hofstadter's book is, to put it into layman's terms, about artificial intelligence. He examines human problem-solving skills and suggests ways in which computer programs can be created that reflect the characteristics of human intelligence – so that computers can 'think' more like us, in other words.

Science fiction, always slightly ahead of the curve, had already begun to explore the implications of all this. What if machines were more like us? The concerns voiced in Karel Čapek's robot play of 1920 had given way to bleak visions of the future in films such as *The Terminator* (the initiator of the so-called 'Tech Noir' genre), and the novels of cyberpunk pioneers like John Brunner, Vernor Vinge and William Gibson. Gibson is credited with coining the word 'cyberspace' in his 1982 story 'Burning Chrome', and he certainly popularized it. His seminal 1984 novel *Neuromancer* would pave the way for *The Matrix* but would also foreshadow our modern relationship with the internet. So it is quite fitting that Hofstadter's book, which discusses the intersections between human and artificial intelligence, and between us and the machines we have invented, became the inaugural purchase on the world's most popular book website.

You may recall that I began the first entry in this book by mentioning the Amazons described by Homer in what is effectively Western civilization's first book. So it seemed fitting to end our library tour with the first book sold on a site with such a classical-sounding name. 'Amazon' may have changed its meaning in the intervening thirty or so centuries, and the physical design of the book may have evolved, but one thing remains constant: books of one kind or another are still a treasured part of our culture.

Here's to the next three thousand years.

# ACKNOWLEDGEMENTS

Writing this book was great fun, and that's largely thanks to the following people. I am grateful to the marvellous team at Michael O'Mara, especially Hugh Barker, Ana McLaughlin and Gabby Nemeth, for their help and support throughout. I would also like to thank the many readers and followers of my blog *Interesting Literature* ('a library of literary interestingness') and Twitter feed, @InterestingLit, for being such a wonderful community of book-lovers and for being partners in procrastination. And finally, thanks to my parents, my brother Matthew, and Rachel. And to Ella – 'the Interesting Literature cat'.

# INDEX

# INDEX